FOR EVERYTHING A SEASON

For
Everything
a Season

Joan Chittister

ORBIS BOOKS
Maryknoll, New York 10545

Founded in 1970, Orbis Books endeavors to publish works that enlighten the mind, nourish the spirit, and challenge the conscience. The publishing arm of the Maryknoll Fathers and Brothers, Orbis seeks to explore the global dimensions of the Christian faith and mission, to invite dialogue with diverse cultures and religious traditions, and to serve the cause of reconciliation and peace. The books published reflect the views of their authors and do not represent the official position of the Maryknoll Society. To learn more about Maryknoll and Orbis Books, please visit our website at www.maryknollsociety.org.

Library of Congress Cataloging-in-Publication Data
Chittister, Joan.
For everything a season / Joan Chittister.
    pages cm
    ISBN 978-1-62698-019-8 (pbk.)
    1. Bible. O.T. Ecclesiastes III, 1-8—Meditations. I. Title.
BS1475.54.C48 2013
242'.5—dc23
                        2012036656

For everything there is a season, and a time for every
matter under heaven:
a time to be born, and a time to die;
a time to plant, and a time to pluck up
what is planted;
a time to kill, and a time to heal;
a time to break down, and a time to build up;
a time to weep, and a time to laugh;
a time to mourn, and a time to dance;
a time to throw away stones, and a time to
gather stones together;
a time to embrace, and a time to
refrain from embracing;
a time to seek, and a time to lose;
a time to keep, and a time to throw away;
a time to tear, and a time to sew;
a time to keep silence, and a time to speak;
a time to love, and a time to hate;
a time for war, and a time for peace . . .

ECCLESIASTES 3:1–8

This book is dedicated to Bill and Betsy Vorsheck
whose continuing support made it possible.
I have seen in them proof of the gilding
that comes in every season of life
and it has touched my own.
I am grateful.

—JOAN CHITTISTER

CONTENTS

Acknowledgments

The seasons of a life are a series of interlocking experiences that, in the end, bring wholeness, breadth of insight, layers of meaning, truth. The seasons of a book are much the same. There are various phases to the process of writing, all of them equally important to the end result, equally shaping the final message. I am equally grateful for them all.

I am, of course, grateful to the artist John August Swanson, whose serigraph *Ecclesiastes* inspired the original edition of this work. Whatever the effect of his work on anyone else, it has had a deep and meaningful effect on me.

I am grateful to Susan Perry and Robert Ellsberg at Orbis, who have given leadership and direction in the presentation of this material.

I am grateful to the body of readers who have so intently and faithfully tested these soundings of life against their own. Marlene Bertke, OSB, Kathleen Hartsell Stephens, Mary Lou Kownacki, OSB, Mary Lee Farrell, GNSH, Stephanie Campbell, OSB, Bro. Thomas Bezanson, and Mary Ann Luke, OSB, in particular, provided important technical and editorial help. Their remarks, suggestions, and questions have strengthened the work.

I am grateful to Bill and Betsy Vorsheck, who gave me the

space and time to bring this work to light.

I am grateful to Marianne Benkert and to A. Richard Sipe, who brought order and quiet to its ending.

I am most grateful of all to Maureen Tobin, OSB, and Mary Grace Hanes, OSB, whose hours of personal support and organizational expertise enabled me to live the multiple lives it takes to write a book and go on functioning as a somewhat useful human being at the same time.

I am no less grateful to those other special people in my life from whom I have learned the truth of these insights and in whom I see the proof and sense the power of a life well lived.

Everyone should have to write this book once in their lives. Working through this topic, wrestling with these ideas, would make their own lives all the more apparent and precious to them, perhaps, as it has to mine.

THE SEASONS
OF LIFE

Like most other people, I suppose, who had been brought up on Scripture or trained in literature, I had heard the words to the point of not hearing them at all: "There is a time to sow, a time to reap; a time for war, a time for peace; a time to heal; a time to kill." Yes, yes, of course. And so?

But as the years went by, I began to notice that with every new year the words took on a timbre I had not heard before; the ideas sprang to meaning in a new way, a new form. Life with all its complexity made it very clear: life is not a drama made up of isolated scenes, each of which is meant to be resolved once and for all. Instead, I came eventually to realize, life is a series of experiences, all of them important, all of them here to be plumbed and squeezed and sucked dry, not for their own sake but so that we may come to know ourselves. Life is not what we see happening on the outside. Life is what goes on inside in the quiet, murky waters of our souls. And life is driven by energies too wild for us to ignore, too deep for us to hide. Life is the bubble of time in which we find ourselves and which we ourselves shape. The insight holds a terrible truth. We are our own captors.

Whatever you are doing right now is mirage. It is not really what you are doing at all. It only looks like it is. Underneath the job, the marriage, the education, the responsibilities that consume the present moment lies the magnet that really draws us on. Each of us, underneath the facades of life, in the bottomless center of ourselves, can, if we listen, hear the sirens cry. They enchant us, seduce us, tempt us, promise us that there is more to life than what we now have. Most of all, they tell us over and over, the more is within our grasp. Each of us lives, then, striving for an invisible finish line, a sun-covered summit, a grail in life that, once we reach it, we are certain will bring with it not only present satisfaction but perpetual peace as well. We live wanting to get it right. We go on searching for the secret to having it all.

We want the medal or the trophy, the job or the house, the money or the recognition, the person or the promotion. Whatever we want we want it badly, and we want it all. We want it now, and we want it forever. We work to the point of exhaustion to get it, or we lounge listlessly through life sure of its existence but unsure of the secret to its capture. We measure ourselves by its existence, or we envy it in someone else. We taste its lack night and day, and we deplete ourselves by the noxious exercise of constantly measuring ourselves against others. It reminds us of our inadequacy, or it lulls us into a sense of slippery superiority. We are looking for life. The problem with life is that it flows and is not graspable. The beauty of life is that it runs and does not stop.

The consequences of such a situation, however, are mixed. In a world made up of ebbs and flows, flux and change, we never really achieve; we only sample. At the same time, if that is the case, it is equally true that we can never be trapped by anything. Because nothing is permanent, nothing is deadly. Life becomes a series of lurches and turns that we struggle to negotiate by redirecting ourselves from one dead-end to another until, finally, we come to see the links between them. Finally, the pattern emerges; finally the very private, very personal edifice of our very separate lives takes shape; finally, the truth dawns that life is simply a matter of living from one season to the next and, if we are lucky, learning as we go.

The proverb teaches: "No one is more unhappy than the one who is never in adversity; the greatest affliction of life is never to be afflicted at all." The question is, of course, is that true? Should that be true? Is perpetual solace not only unattainable but undesirable as well? And if so, why? The answers do not come easily.

Ironically enough, the vagaries of life move us on surely as much as its blessings, and sometimes more so. Death, unexpected and paralyzing or expected and draining, demands of us new ingress into life. Failure, garnered heroically or earned by stubborn stupidity, requires us to begin again. Loss, suffered because of circumstances outside of us or mandated by that inadequacy within us that has been tested beyond its level, compels us to start over. Life is not lived in a straight line. Life comes out of nowhere, or at least out of where we would rather not be, again and again and again.

The tension lies in being able to let go of the past. In a society of strivers, however, enough is never enough. In an achievement-driven society, life is not a thing of seasons; life is a product to be perfected and preserved. To this mind, it is never possible to simply go on, past the things of the past to the realities of the present. No, those who live by measuring sticks rather than by the meaning of the present moment are intent on gaining and grasping. Letting go is not virtue to them. Letting go is loss. They hold on. And why not? It is often more comfortable to board up the windows of the soul after a death than it is to venture out into the light alone again. It is sometimes more comfortable to crawl into a corner after failure and refuse to try again than it is to bear the stares of those who saw the shabby first effort. It is certainly less painful, less disruptive, to surrender to the limiting expectations of those around us than it is to shape for ourselves a larger, broader world. It is so much easier to maintain someone else's definition of perfect wife, for instance, than it is to demand to be peer and professional, easier to be the corporate lackey than inventor, easier to wear the uniform of the socially acceptable than to eat locusts and wild honey.

There is a another kind of tension far beyond adversity, however. Adversity, at least, gets our attention. But joy we take for granted. Joy we consider birthright and wait to inherit in outrageous proportions. Yet, joy we too often ignore. As a result, joy unheeded and blessings unacknowledged carry serious psychological and spiritual significance of their own for us. Henry Ward Beecher knew it well. "There are joys," he wrote, "which long to be ours. God sends ten thousand truths, which come about us like birds seeking inlet; but we are shut up to them, and so they bring us nothing, but sit and sing awhile upon the roof, and then fly away."

But joy is the spirit of God in time. It is the only taste of eternity that is freely given. We have, in other words, cultivated our capacity to slight life. Joy is the energy to carry on through dull days knowing that miracles can happen in the future because we have seen them in the past.

Finally, tension lies, too, in being willing to engage the present. Being where we are—immersed in it, aware of it, alert to it—may well be the secret to living well, to living fully. It is a lesson to be learned. In a culture based on motion it is no small trick to allow ourselves to be present to the present, to see what is in front of us.

We only think we're here. The problem is a perennial one, common to every time, every tradition, noted in story form by many:

"Where shall I look for Enlightenment?" the disciple asked.

"Here," the elder said.

"When will it happen?" the disciple asked.

"It is happening right now," the elder answered. "Then why don't I experience it?" the disciple persisted.

"Because you do not look," the elder said.

"But what should I look for?" the disciple continued.

"Nothing. Just look," the elder said.

"But at what?" the disciple asked again.

"At anything your eyes alight upon," the elder answered.

"But must I look in a special kind of way?" the disciple went on.

"No. The ordinary way will do," the elder said. "But don't I always look the ordinary way?" the disciple said.

"No, you don't," the elder said.

"But why ever not?" the disciple asked.

"Because to look you must be here. You're mostly somewhere else," the elder said.

In too many instances, we are really more likely to be on our way to somewhere else than present to the present. We go through life watching our watches. We leave one party early in order to go to another one, and by the end of the night we have enjoyed neither. We live with one foot in tomorrow at all times. We plan for tomorrow and prepare for tomorrow and fear tomorrow and wait for tomorrow with distracting fitfulness. Here is never good enough. What is, is not important to a people on the go. What is coming is always what really counts. What is yet to be had, yet to be seen, yet to be done, yet to be accomplished becomes the essence of life.

But life is every grain of sand in the hourglass. And it is running. And once run it is gone forever.

Too often, while we wait for life, it passes us by, leaves us up to our hearts in dissatisfaction and over our heads in wanting. We live overcome by losses and dissolved in spiritual ruin or wasted by a dearth of spirit, by a diminishment of enthusiasm, by the dissipation of hope. Yet all the while the present moment lies richly dormant within us.

The Book of Ecclesiastes, one of the Wisdom books of the Hebrew-Christian Scriptures, is an antidote to the problem of aimlessness and disorientation, of personal fragmentation and nagging despair. Ecclesiastes invites us to see life as a mosaic made up of small pieces of human experience common to us all but lived uniquely by each one of us. Ecclesiastes calls us to the universals of life so that we can understand it before we lose it, enjoy it before we miss it.

The fundamental problem of life, obviously, is not a lack of opportunity. It is a lack of soul, of what Confucians call "righteousness," of what Buddhists call "awareness," of what Jews call "tsedakah," of what Christians call "contemplative consciousness."

The purpose of this book is to plumb clearly and consciously the words of Ecclesiastes, with the eyes of the untutored, to learn from them, to inscribe them on our hearts, to allow ourselves to be questioned by them so that, if and when we find ourselves at these same moments in life again, we may be there this time with fresh and open hearts. The portions of a person's life they strew before our eyes with a kind of reckless abandon. "Here," they shout, "What you do not understand in your own life consider again. Look newly. Look at life once more, and where you have been blinded, see, and where you have become numb to the point of the senseless, the dead of heart, now glory."

A Time to
Be Born

Ecclesiastes is quite clear: the first thing a person is meant to understand is that there is no such thing as being "born out of time." Our time is now. The era into which we are born is the era for which we have responsibility, the era for which we are meant to be blessing. The implications are sobering. Whatever is going on now—ethnic slaughter, unjust international business policies, the false god of militarism, the sexism of the churches—is our affair. What we want to have happen in these arenas we must make happen in our own.

William Jennings Bryan said it well: "Destiny is no matter of chance. It is a matter of choice: It is not a thing to be waited for, it is a thing to be achieved." But if that is true, then destiny is a thing to be consciously grasped, not something to be suffered unawares. More than that, perhaps, destiny has something to do with discovering what we ought to be doing. It has something to do with shaping our way of being in the world. We do not live like crustaceans on a seawall, simply lapping up the water and absorbing plankton. We live with a larger purpose, with something expected of us, with a sense of connectedness to the rest of life, not like hothouse plants, attended but never rooted in an environment bigger than themselves. Destiny is the enemy of selfishness.

Privatism, pietism, and psychology have sanctified the sin of individualism. And it has not all been bad. We have learned, after all, to see in this generation what has never been seen before. We have discovered individual differences, and we have provided for individual needs. We have protected individual rights and bathed in individual exceptions. It has been a time of personal spotlights and personal choice. We have atomized society to the level of its least common denominators, and while we were doing it, we fragmented the community mind.

People feel isolated now. Like automatons in a silent sea we pass one another in the dark, groping our way along without mooring and without restraint. No one touches anyone. We work for years with people whose last names we do not know. We live in buildings for years with people we have never met. We form "support groups" made up of strangers to help put all the pieces back together again. In the place of the group, we have put the person, vulnerable, insulated, and alone. Very alone.

We have never had a more literate population or a more powerless one. Now the best-educated people in the history of the world do not know what to do with what they know.

Everything is too big for us, too overwhelming for us, too global for us. So we "mind our own business" and ignore everything else. We have learned well not to see the bodies that we step over in the streets or the elderly ill in the neighborhood. They are all the responsibility of someone else—of bureaus and agencies and faceless civil servants. We have handed conscience over to government programs and looked away.

Personal development, not personal responsibility, is the high priest of the age. Nothing must interfere with my personal comfort. Nothing may take precedence. It is a pernicious disease and it has sickened our society. The philosophy has invaded our schools and invaded the workplace and eroded the foundations of our social institutions. Now no one can expect from anyone anything more than that person's own best interests.

The question is, what will reverse this trend toward pathological personalism? What can possibly fill the gap between extreme individualism and group mindlessness so that we can know the community conscience and save the community soul?

According to Ecclesiastes it is the sense of ownership that falls to those who face the fact that this is our time to be born, that it is up to us now to choose our destinies in it. Just as once it was Pavel's time in Hungary and Mandela's time in South Africa and Mary Robinson's time in Ireland—all simple people who emerged against impossible odds—it is my time right here, in this tiny city right now. What happens here now is my responsibility. What happens tomorrow is my legacy to it. It is not a matter of doing great things. No, it is far worse than that. It is a matter of doing small things courageously.

It takes great courage to disagree with government policies in polite company. It takes great courage to admit I am a feminist when women are being ridiculed. It takes great courage to oppose militarism on the Fourth of July. Those are the modest acts of principle that make the doing of the impious impossible.

Modest, perhaps. But not uncomplicated. Not to be taken lightly. Before we face the world around us, we must first face ourselves. Character clear as blue crystal has to be born in us before we can begin to do what we were born to do for others. I think often of the Confucian scholar Qian Dehong.

"Why can't I influence other people?" his student asked him.

And Master Qian said, "As soon as you speak of influencing other people, this is already not right. The sages just made themselves correct and others spontaneously corrected themselves. For example," he went on, "when the sun is uncovered, its light can shine on things. It does not have to make a special effort to go looking for things to shine on."

The question is, what is it in us that makes us reluctant to let the light shine?

There are three obstacles to the development in us of the force of personality that would make us a moral factor in the world around us:

First, fear of loss of status has done more to chill character than history will ever know. We do not curry favor with kings by pointing out that the emperor has no clothes. We do not gain promotions by countering the beloved viewpoints of the chair of the board or the bishop of the diocese. We do not get invited to house and garden parties by being politically incorrect. We do not figure in the neighborhood barbecues if we embarrass the Pentagon employees in the gathering by a public commitment to demilitarization. It is hard time, this choice of destiny between public conscience and social acceptability. Then we tell ourselves that nothing is to be gained by upsetting people. And sure enough, nothing is.

Second, personal comfort is a factor, too, in the decision to let other people bear responsibility for the tenor of our times. It takes a great deal of effort to turn my attention beyond the confines of where I work and where I live and what my children do. It lies in registering interest in something beyond my small, small world and perhaps taking part in group discussions or lectures. It requires turning my mind to substance beyond the sitcoms and the sports channel and the local weekly. It means not allowing myself to go brain-dead before the age of forty. But these things that cost comfort are exactly the things that will, ultimately, make life better for my work and my children.

Third, fear of criticism is no small part, surely, of this unwillingness to be born into the world for which I have been born. To differ from the mainstream of humanity, to take a position that is not popular on a topic that is not acceptable tests the tenor of the best of debaters, the strongest of thinkers, the most skilled of speakers. To do that at the kitchen table, in the office, at the family table takes the utmost in courage, the ultimate in love, the keenest of communication skills. And who of us think we have them?

The process of human discourse is a risky one. Other people speak more clearly or convincingly than we do. Other people have better academic backgrounds than we do. Other people have authority and robes and buttons and titles that we do not now and never will have, and to confront those things takes nerve of a special gauge. I may lose. I may make a perfect fool out of myself. But everybody has to be perfect about something. What else can be more worth it than giving the gift of the perfect question in a world uncomfortable with the answers but too frightened or too complacent or too ambitious to raise these doubts again?

I have no doubt, however, that the courage to ask questions is part of what it takes to give birth to a soul of crystal. In fact, I have seen the proof of it.

It was Mother's Day in a small-town church. Everything was as it should be. The children were scrubbed to a sheen. The women wore corsages. Men who hadn't been to church for months were in the pews. The nuns sang special hymns, and the priest had a special homily prepared. Before he could begin, however, a woman stood up in the middle of the chapel and called out loud and clear,

"Why is a man giving this homily? It's Mother's Day. No man should be giving the homily. A woman should."

The congregation sat stunned and uneasy. The priest cleared his throat to begin again. The woman stood up one more time. "I have something to read," she said and recited a poem about the strength and gifts of women. They escorted, her out of the church, of course, soothing her all the way.

They told the story for days, a little nervously, a little shocked. But no one has forgotten the incident. No one has forgotten the question. After two thousand years of sitting quietly through improper repression, they were stunned by the impropriety of a woman who risked status, comfort, and criticism to name it aloud while she mothered the women of the world. But I have an idea that no one has forgotten the message or ever will. And who knows? Maybe, because of it, something new was born that day in that church that will someday, finally, come to light. It was a small act of personal courage, but it should not be taken lightly.

There is, indeed, "a time to be born." It is a spiritual imperative. There is a time to come out of the cocoon of the self so that others may have life.

Difficult as it may be socially, there are great spiritual rewards for taking on the burdens of our time as our own, for living in it full of integrity, empty of guile. We become the women and men we are capable of being. We become the parents we should be. We become spiritually adult.

They criticized the woman who cried out in church for women on Mother's Day, but I remembered Jesus, too, raging in a temple that spoke of God's mercy and then wreaked injustice on the poor. They said she should never have made such "a public spectacle of her protest" in front of her children because it gave them a bad example. But I don't know. Maybe what their mother did is the best example they'll ever get of taking ridicule for the sake of her faith. They said the woman "should never have embarrassed the priest that way" in public, but maybe, just maybe, the only way the public invisibility of women will ever come to an end is for everyone else to feel the same kind of embarrassment for their existence as women do.

One thing for sure, the woman had the spiritual gifts that come from taking seriously that the time we are born into is the time for us to be born, the time that is waiting for us and our gifts, the time that is ours to give our life to saving. She had freedom and she had self-esteem. She had what we all need to meet the hollows and peaks of the period in which we live. Without the inner freedom it takes to defy the chains of convention, without the self-esteem it takes to trust our own truth, we face our worlds unprepared and unaware.

Freedom is the capstone of truth. Our time is short here and there is much to do. Therefore, we must cultivate a passion for the truth. We must seek it, demand it, and tell it. And once we have broken through the levels of propriety and protocol that collude to pretend that what isn't true is necessary, we are forever free. No one can ever enslave us again.

Self-esteem is the blessing that comes with honesty. With self-esteem we cannot lose, no matter what we lose. Longfellow's lines hold immortal value: "Those that respect themselves are safe from others; they wear a coat of mail that none can pierce." When we have done what must be done, what we were put here to do at this time, in this age, at this place, then we can live with heads up and hearts unbroken, whatever our losses. Then no one can best us, even when we fail the fray. Then we will never die before we have lived.

This time, indeed, is my only time to be born. On it, in fact, depend the two pillars of my life: my freedom of soul and my eternal self-esteem.

A Time to Lose

In his seriagraph of the text from Ecclesiastes the artist John August Swanson illustrates the panel, "A Time to Lose," with an image of Adam and Eve being banished from the Garden of Eden. "A Time to Lose"? Well, that was not the way my second-grade teacher saw it at all. When Adam and Eve were turned out of Eden it was not, as far as she was concerned, a situation to be defined at the level of a "loss." It was in the style of disgrace and shame and total human degradation. Thanks to them, thanks to their mindless and miserable failure, she taught, nothing had ever been right since. For any of us. In one fell swoop, she insisted, we had squandered it all. No, Sister Laura would not have called the painting, "A Time to Lose," as if this were just another one of life's little processes. She would surely have called it, "A Time to Be Punished" or a "A Time to Repent" or something, at least, that brooked no doubt about the fact that this was a mess and who was at fault for it and what ought to be done about it. Sister Laura was a purist.

I thought about that scene for years. And as time went by I began to think Sister Laura may have missed something and in missing it blinded me for years as well. Thanks to that kind of theology, I had grown up under the impulse of another set of meanings and another set of labels. As a result of that kind of thinking, I saw all failure as bad. Like a child who stumbles into the family heirloom and breaks it, I felt full of sin instead of full of promise. I had as a result been able to miss completely the church's more certain concept, sung in the ecstatic *Exultet* of Easter night, when finally Adam and Eve get their share of praise. "Oh, happy fault" the church, full-throated, sings. "Oh, happy fault," that brought us the need for such a savior. "Oh, happy fault" that brought us to this point.

"No evil is without its compensation," the Roman rhetorician Seneca wrote. "The less money, the less trouble; the less favor, the less envy." Nothing, in other words, is all bad.

The Chinese tell a charming story about a farmer who had only one plow horse to get him through planting time. One day the horse broke away from his stake and ran off into the hills. Neighbors poured in to commiserate with the man's bad luck. "Well, good event, bad event," the farmer responded. "Who knows?"

And sure enough a few weeks later, the horse came galloping down the mountain leading an entire pack of wild horses straight into the open corral. The neighbors went wild with glee. "Well," the old man said in quiet answer to their excited congratulations, "good event, bad event. Who knows?"

And sure enough at harvest time, the farmer's only son and heir fell under the bucking horse he was training and suffered a totally mangled leg. The neighbors were beside themselves with distress for the aging man, whose harvest was now in danger. "Well, good event, bad event. Who knows?" The old man shrugged as he saw most of his harvest lost in the field.

Then about six weeks later, the warlord came through the valley, conscripting every young man in the village for the latest feudal war. With one exception. The warlord would not have the crippled son of the aging farmer as part of the king's noble army. And when his neighbors, grieving for the loss of their own sons, envied the old farmer for the presence of his, he simply folded his hands and said, "Well, good event, bad event. Who knows?"

That fact is that loss is not only, not always, bad, but also is sometimes great good in disguise. The United States never lost a war, for instance, until it crumbled in front of a Vietnamese guerrilla army, and then, for the first time, war became a less certain foreign policy than ever before in the history of the country. If the young Indian lawyer Mohandas Gandhi had not been thrown off a train in South Africa because he was colored, it is probable that the movement that became known as nonviolent resistance would never have developed. Yet without it, India itself may not have won its independence from England for years nor may the United States have ever known its own nonviolent Civil Rights movement that developed under that same impetus here as well. If Helen Keller had not been deaf, the whole deaf world might still be tortured by silence.

And in our own simple lives so many losses weave the skein of reality. The death of the father becomes the beginning of a whole new life for everyone in the family. The loss of the job becomes the beginning of the new and better career. The end of the money means the opportunity to extricate ourselves from the counterfeit lifestyle that had sedated our minds and plasticized our souls. Loss is surely meant to be an invitation to options.

For those who know loss, life cries out for fulfillment, and possibility is forever new.

Learning the value of loss is, however, a trip to a foreign land. Loss galls the spirit of this culture to the bone. We do not teach our children to lose. We teach them how to lose. We teach them the rituals of losing, that is, but we do not teach them the role of losing in life.

In this world, we learn quickly that losing is failure rather than simply another way to a different goal. Everything we learn from infancy on is intended to be tested to determine our capacity for success and our ability to compete. None of it has much to do at all with our talent for life itself.

We do not teach the children of this culture that games are games, for instance. We teach our children that games are life. We say that games shape character and build confidence, and then if they are students we bribe them to play for us and pad their grades. If they are professionals, we pay them obscene amounts of money to win for us and then fine them for using the drugs or instigating the brawls that our need to win demands of them. And all the while we line up our young for handshakes and snacks after the game, we whisper in their ears that "no one remembers who came in second" and that "winning isn't everything, it's the only thing."

Then we wonder why suicide and divorce and wife-beating statistics are so high after economic downswings. We lament the fact that welfare families stop trying to get ahead. We can't imagine the degree of white-collar crime that has emerged to cover up financial mistakes and business errors and social embarrassments. We rue widowhood and corporate changes and broken plans like the plague. The game is to win—and everything is the game.

We have forgotten the virtue of losing. We have destroyed the creativity of loss. We have turned the natural cycle of learning by failing into shame and guilt and anger.

But that is not what the Garden of Eden was all about. "What God gave Adam," Elie Wiesel wrote, "was not forgiveness from sin. What God gave Adam was the right to begin again." If we want to be mentally healthy, if we want to live full and vibrant lives, we need to remember the lesson of the Garden of Eden. It is the fine art of learning to be wrong.

Loss can be a lovely and freeing thing. It gives to a few what is too often missing to the many. It provides a chance for a person to start over in life, to scrape away the barnacles of time and empty out the accretions of the years. It says there is in us whatever it takes to learn from the past and adapt to the future. It says that resilience is a grace for the asking.

There are two hurdles to be overcome in us if loss is ever to be the elixir of life that it was meant to be. The first barrier to the liberating experience of loss is the need to succeed. The second barrier is the corruption that comes with the need to control.

The question, of course, is a basic one: Did Adam and Eve, our archetypes of the human race, succeed or fail? The answer, I think, depends on whether we think of them as human or divine. If we see them as quasi-divine, then they were, indeed, failures of the most monstrous kind, aware of truth and disregarding of it, in touch with the heights and uncaring of them. Impetuous imposters both, they were beneath the gods and an embarrassment to the human race as well. The fact is, however, that Eve and Adam were human, not angelic, and the eating of the apple was the most humanizing thing they did. What if the real message in the Garden story is that it is of the essence of humanity to stumble from apple tree to apple tree, trying to get it right, searching for "the difference between good and evil" but able to learn it only the hard way? Then the lesson for the human race to learn from the Garden was not that God was angry that Adam and Eve were not gods but that God knew it was necessary for them to learn that they were human, that life would not be easy, that there would be pitfalls aplenty, and most of all, that they could survive them one after the other after the other.

Success, Ecclesiastes implies, is not the ability to maintain good fortune; it is the ability to survive loss. It is, in fact, the redefinition of success that loss brings to life on gilded wings.

The second barrier to understanding the value of loss may be the hardest one of all to negotiate. The loss of the sense of self that defeat brings in its wake is the struggle we cannot name and the devil we cannot rout. If I do not get the trophy, am I a real athlete at all? If I lose the promotion, is there anything left of me to present to the public? If I have no achievements, no hoard of treasures, no list of titles, no host to which to append myself, am I really anything at all? How does a divorcée face the city? How does the widow begin to go out alone? How does the past president face the world? How does the college dropout face the neighborhood? How does the defeated quarterback face the family that schooled him to win? How do people redefine themselves after loss? The answer, of course, is in Ecclesiastes. We must redefine ourselves just as Adam and Eve did—as Adam and Eve, the same people, but wiser now and open to the promise of new life.

The spiritual effects of loss are profound. We come to know ourselves in the contests we could not win and the summits we could not scale and the goals we could not reach and in the loss of loves we could not live without. Then, like Adam and Eve, driven from the Edens of our life by the inadequacies of our soul, we come to see who we really are and what we're really made of. And we're amazed. We find that we have the ability to suffer as well as the ability to win, and we realize, then, that we can never really lose again. We can be made to do with less than once we had or dreamed about or wanted, perhaps, but we can never be made to believe that life dies when things die or people go or images fade or the world turns one more uncontrollable time.

Self-knowledge is what happens when we find out that what we cannot do is not the only thing we can do. We cannot be an actor, perhaps, and so we fail to get the part, but we can paint scenery and so we become a designer. We cannot be the executive of the organization and are not given the position we wanted, but we can be its mainstay. We cannot be a great artist and no one buys our paintings, but we can put beauty in every poor and squalid room we enter.

And so we grow to full stature, not by always winning but by often losing. The Confucian scholar Ouyang De taught, "The water at the source and the water downstream are not two different natures. . . . All that we see and hear and think and do is due to heaven. All we have to do is to recognize what is true and what is false."

What is true is that we ourselves are more than however much we strive to achieve. What is false is that losing anything will be the end of us. What is true is that losing something can, in fact, be the beginning of an exciting new world, a totally new life, a completely different and even more satisfying way of being. What is real is that the water at the source and the water downstream are not two different natures. Whatever we are when our great life changes come is what we shall take into the next phase of life.

Things and positions and titles do not make us; we make them. No person in a position is one bit more than they ever were out of it, and being out of a position does not diminish us at all. What we did not have before we discovered the diamonds we will not be when we find them. A fool with a diamond is nothing but a fool with a diamond.

"The art of losing isn't hard to master," Elizabeth Bishop wrote. "So many things seem filled with the intent to be lost that their loss is no disaster." Loss is simply another entrance into life. Whatever we are not prepared to lose we are enslaved to maintain—at any cost. Whatever we are not prepared to lose diminishes our sense of soul and depth of spirit. This definition of life is too narrow to nurture, too dangerous to maintain. It is time to lose it.

A Time to Love

Thornton Wilder may have already said much of all there is to say on the subject. He wrote, "There is a land of the living and a land of the dead and the bridge is love, the only survival, the only meaning." What Wilder did not say is that it is so easy to rhapsodize about love, and many people do. It is so easy to fantasize about love, and whole industries are built on it. It is so easy to distort love and call it marriage.

More things pass for love than could substitute for the real item in almost any other category on earth. Sex and marriage and cohabitation all form the charade that has been bought and sold to look like varying degrees of commitment and eternal happiness.

Or put it this way: anything that degrades or demeans or destroys a person in any way is not love, no matter how loudly proclaimed.

Foreign as the concept of love as an exalting experience may be in a world given to premeditated and pernicious violence, it is home to the heart. It is at the same time alien to the point of the exotic now. We live in a culture that abuses its children and calls it love, but such abuse has never developed healthy adults. We live in a society that looks benignly on spousal rape and calls it love, but such heartlessness has never produced a hallowed home. We spawn a public who humiliate one another in the name of "truth" until people shrivel in embarrassment, and we call it tough love, but degradation has never ended in holy friendship. We need to look at love again.

Sex drives this culture, not love. Because we cannot deny the feminist truth that women at large are treated like objects for male satisfaction and male service, we now deride feminism itself as brazen and crazy and unnatural and loud, a delusional relative shouting "Fire!" in the shower. But the statistics are all there shouting "Lie!" for those who are willing to see. We pay women less than we pay men in every single category in which they are employed, except prostitution and modeling, and say we respect them. We give them fancy titles now—Associate Director to the President, perhaps—but go on using them like clerks and say we revere them. We take their ideas but pass them over for promotions and say we value them. We trivialize their health problems but charge them more for health insurance and say we care for them. We say God made them equal to men but don't want them around churches, and we say we look to them for moral leadership but don't give them any. We confuse biology and gender roles, using one to define the other and say we see them as whole persons. We interpret mothering as eternally determinative but define fathering as a fleeting event and say there is no difference between our expectations of fatherhood and our demands on motherhood. We put a token woman on every committee in order to keep the rest of the women off of it and say we believe in equality. We tut-tut women and patronize women and put women down and call it "God's will for them." And then we say how much we love them.

But that is not love. That is sexism. That does not make royalty of any of us. No real marriage can possibly be built on that kind of human misuse. No sanctifying friendship between the sexes can possibly rest on that foundation. That is diminishment of half the human race, and it is acid on the soul of men as well.

Sexism has stunted the development of men as surely as it has blocked the development of women. Men are victimized to the point of the absurd by it. If they do not want to brutalize other human beings for sport or social policy, they are ostracized for being weak. If money is not their only goal in life, they are labeled unsuccessful. If as children they begin to show emotion, they are told to "act like little men" and then find that they have no life-saving emotions left to retrieve when they grow up. They are told to be responsible for people who, in many instances, are smarter than they are. So, because they cannot do it and dare not say they cannot do it, they find themselves nagged and ridiculed all their inadequate lives. Then in their frustration they become bullies and batterers to prove their manliness. And, finally, they die young from overwork and overworry and overreaching.

We put women on pedestals and men in positions, but plastic pedestals and profiteering positions are no substitute for personhood. Being allowed to be half a person is no reward. Being seduced into the limitations of sexism is advantageous to some of us but diminishing of all of us. Marriage and machoism, pornography and passion, domination and partnership are not synonyms. But we go on selling sex and sexism and all in the name of love.

Love that is more real than self-satisfying exalts a person not to the heights of the unattainably romanticized, but to the level of the beautiful and the real. Love that does not free each of us to become our best and fullest selves befriends neither person and defrauds both. It is dishonesty so basic that no amount of marriage counseling, no patina of personal propriety, can ever cure its corrosion. The man who gets married to have someone take care of him, who wants "an old-fashioned wife" whose role in life is to live for him alone, does not really love anyone but himself. The best of them buy it with candy and flowers, but they are buying, nevertheless. The woman who wants to "marry a doctor" so that she can have a nice home and plenty of money reduces a man to the level of domestic help and marriage to a business agreement, no matter how well she plays its social game.

Love is about regal respect, royal reverence, and total support. It needs to be taught rather than made the victim of a kind of hormonal roulette. Chemistry quickens love, but it does not prove it, and it will not sustain it.

Love, unfortunately for those who simplify it to their peril, is a paradox. It requires total commitment to the well-being of the other, and it demands total commitment to the well-being of the self as well. We teach devotion to the other but we do not understand that development of the self is equally important if there is to be any real relationship at all. We applaud one and are embarrassed by the other. Consequently, we teach little about love that is valid at all.

Love resides in the sanctification of friendship. Sad news, indeed, for those who have been sacrificed to the smoke screen of physical attraction or social status where heart and single-mindedness should have been. Friendship, a subject of great philosophical inquiry to the ancients, lies chloroformed in the Western soul under the pose of companionship, teamwork, and social nicety. We have garbled the word to the point that it says almost nothing at all. No survival, no meaning, no royal commitment here. Friendship is sterner stuff than that.

Friendship requires the meeting of equals. "Friendship is one mind in two bodies," the poet Mencius wrote. Friendship bursts with the electric excitement that comes when we recognize a mind that is the mirror of our own, not its echo, not its opposite but not its muffler either. Equality and synergy become the touchstones of friendship, the measure of its meaning, the silken thread of survival that is its warp and woof.

I look to a friend for tender support and tough truth. I give a friend my attention and my interest, my genuine care, my deepest concern. I find in a friend's look that I am attractive and in a friend's laughter that I am engaging and in a friend's responses that I have something of value to say. I see in a friend someone I respect for qualities I admire and someone who, however surprising I find it, respects me for gifts I have trouble seeing in myself. I feel my own quality in the presence of a sterling friend.

A friend is not an interruption in life. A friend is the glue of my life, the centerpoint that holds all the rest of it together and assesses it for substance. Friendship is a game of high standards and wild excess where everything is possible, but only the best in both of us meets the test of the acceptable. Friends do not frown; they question. Friends do not block; they enable. Friends do not control; they stand by. Friends do not dominate; they foster the best in me until no dross remains. Friends do not smother me; they free me. Friends do not love me for their sake; they love me for my sake. They love me the way I want to be loved, not the way they want to love me. A friend is the other side of my soul.

Where there is no friend, there is no real conversation, there is only talk. Where there is no friend, there is no trusted counselor, only temporary listeners, basically distracted and essentially uninterested. Where there is no friend, there may be people aplenty who need my service, but there is no one there because of whom life is glorious for me and dying is impossible.

The loss of a friend is not a gap in the environment; it is a gouge in the heart forever. Nothing replaces a lost friend because when a friend goes, a door in my own life closes that can never be opened by anyone else again. The poet William Blake knew the problem well, I think. He wrote, "Thy friendship oft has made my heart to ache; do be my enemy—for friendship's sake."

Without friendship, life limps along on the mechanics of love but lacks its soul.

Friendship can exist in marriage, that is true. But what is dangerously more true is that marriage cannot exist without friendship even if that marriage never ends. Friendship is what we need to know about marriage. When the chemistry changes and the honeymoon turns to the mortgage, if there is no friendship, there is no marriage. Time won't do it. Children won't do it. Traditionalism won't do it. Equality and synergy are the only things that will make a marriage a friendship and make a friendship love.

Two things eat away at the human heart and block the development of love in us. One is narcissism and the other is lack of self-esteem. The narcissists believe, though they would seldom say it, perhaps, that they were born to have people wait on them. This is the man who "helps around the house" and "babysits the kids one night a week so the wife can go out." This is the woman who pouts and whines because "he never does anything nice" for her but never does anything nice for herself either. Making her happy, she thinks, is his job. These people give someone else the responsibility for their lives and consume everything in sight for their own purposes. They take and take and take and give nothing back. They want marriages with "roles" clearly defined to suit them.

The other barrier to holy friendship is low self-esteem. What we do not have within us we do not have to give another. All we can do is to attach ourselves to someone else for refuge or for identity. Neither attachment is enough to deserve an eternity of affection. And so, sooner or later, clearly or imperceptibly, the relationship unravels and is seen for what it is: a skeleton of a partnership. When a marriage is designed so that one life must be lost so that the other can be lived, marriage has become a misnomer for domestication.

Ironically enough then, a friendship that is not independent is not a friendship at all. And more important than that, perhaps, in today's confusion of sex roles and self-development, a marriage that depends on the obliteration of one of the partners is no partnership at all. She is more than a mother; she is a person with talents and ideas. He is more than a provider; he is a man with feelings and fears. A marriage based on friendship provides the possibility for both and stifles neither.

"Marriage," Joseph Barth wrote, "is our last best chance to grow up." It is, in other words, our golden hope for fulfillment in a union that commits but does not bind, that links but does not limit us from becoming the person that each of us was meant to be.

The spiritual effects of love are legion, but three have special meaning. To know love is to know trust that is dizzy and free. Once we have loved one other we are capable of loving the world. Once we have discovered unexpected treasure we presume to find it everywhere. Then love becomes a natural resource, an element of the universe, an energy that I learn to mine from person to person in my life.

But if seeing glory in someone else is our invitation to appreciate the glory in the whole world, then a sense of God's marvels in me is an invitation to understand the meaning of heaven here.

Right here and now. To be loved by someone is to become new again, to know the gleam that comes with being worthwhile, to discover what it is to be wonderful.

"What does your fiancée like about you?" the mother asked her moonstruck son.

"She thinks I'm handsome, talented, clever, and a good dancer," he said dreamily.

"And what do you like about her?" the mother said.

"That she thinks I'm handsome, talented, clever, and a good dancer!" the boy said.

The message is only partially untrue. Love not only saves us from the smallness of ourselves and gives us the courage to risk ourselves on others. Love teaches us as well the grandeur of a God who does miracles through the unlikely likes of a limited me. It gives us esteem, admiration, regard, and respect. Love makes us feel beautiful, feel regal. It lifts us out of the humdrum of the ordinary to crown us with surprise and fullness of life. It brings with it a cataract of approval and pride and affirmation and attention that makes long days easy and hard times possible. Love enables us to love ourselves, the fundamental preparation for being able to love anybody else.

Finally, love shows us into the heart of God. The Hasidic masters tell the story of the rabbi who disappeared every Shabat Eve, "to commune with God in the forest," his congregation thought. So one Sabbath night they deputed one of their cantors to follow the rabbi and observe the holy encounter. Deeper and deeper into the woods the rabbi went until he came to the small cottage of an old Gentile woman, sick to death and crippled into a painful posture. Once there, the rabbi cooked for her and carried her firewood and swept her floor. Then when the chores were finished, he returned immediately to his little house next to the synagogue.

Back in the village, the people demanded of the one they'd sent to follow him, "Did our rabbi go up to heaven as we thought?"

"Oh, no," the cantor answered after a thoughtful pause, "our rabbi went much, much higher than that."

The rabbi's message sears the soul: Love is not for our own sakes. Love frees us to see others as God sees them.

To love is to come to see beyond and despite good taste, good sense, and good judgment. Love sees us as we are, as we really are, and as we can be, as well.

Love sees little but good in us and forgives everything that is not. We watch it happen every day and, from a dry and loveless perch in our desiccated souls, pronounce it ridiculous when, perhaps, we should proclaim it holy. Foolish love, in fact, may be all we ever know of the love of God on earth and, in the end, it will be everything that each of us needs. In the end it will indeed be "the bridge, the survival, the meaning."

A Time to
Laugh

If there were ever proof that the spiritual life, the holy life, is not an exercise in the dour and the depressing, this is certainly it. Ecclesiastes, the Book of Qoheleth, is, I am sure, the bedside reading of few people I know. Here, in other words, is a serious book, a book to be taken seriously, a book not to be taken lightly. So we can trust it, right? Right. And Qoheleth, as baldly as he states that there is "a time to lose," also states that there is a time to laugh. "To everything there is a season," he says. And sometimes it is the season for laughter.

Very sober things have been said about laughter. Some of the most boring essays ever penned have been written in an attempt to dissect laughter or at least to drive it off the face of the earth. Loving laughter as I do, I used to buy those books, certain that they would be good for my digestion as well as my mind. If truth were known, I bought two different volumes of articles on the subject because after I read the first one, I was sure it was a satire that I had not been smart enough to understand. By the time I had finished the second set of essays, though, I knew that I had never in my life been in more socially damaging company. Here was a group of people who could single-handedly take the smile off the face of a clown. Here was malice aforethought parading as benign intent. The academic analysis of laughter, I am absolutely sure, is not what Qoheleth had in mind.

Qoheleth, I think, was talking about that airing of the soul, that breath of the spirit that comes in the irrepressible awareness of the incomprehensible, the impossible, and the disjunctive—a dog who can play cards or a God who cannot play golf. Laughter marks the moment when all the rules of life fail and the world does not end, when the playing field of life is leveled and serfs laugh at kings and queens take pratfalls in farmer's yards, when children confound their parents and the little people of the world win the day.

"Young man," the teacher said, "since you do not think it important to pay attention in this class, please tell us what happened in 1898?"

"The Battleship *Maine* was sunk, Ma'am," the child answered.

"And then what happened in 1900?" the teacher persisted.

"The Battleship *Maine* was sunk for two years, Ma'am."

Suddenly life is glorious again, anything is possible, and defeat is not forever.

Most of all, laughter is healthy when we are able to laugh at ourselves, when making a mistake is more a moment of freedom from protocol than it is one of the hidden tragedies of life. When I am laughing at myself, I have crossed the Rubicon of life and given notice that I can risk being mortal and know I shall survive.

Laughter liberates and laughter uplifts. When laughter comes into a life, nothing is impossible, nothing is too difficult, nothing can defeat us. We can survive the noonday sun and the darkness of death and the grinding boredom of dailiness and still find life exhilarating. Other things in life change character like chameleons on plaid, but laughter is always ornament, always grace.

Some people, of course, are just plain incapable of humor. They start jokes by telling the punch line. Then they end the jokes without one. They tell two jokes at once and never know they've mixed them. They're a sorry but a lovable crowd who can be saved by silence and a funny friend. For them laughter is a blessing, not a simple gift. That's all right. If everyone played the piano, who would buy the records? There are far worse afflictions of the human race. This crowd is, in fact, a boon to humanity. They keep the family dinners worth attending. No matter how many times Uncle Louie tells the same story, year after year, they laugh. We need them more than gold.

Some people, on the other hand, are humorless. Either they haven't cultivated the virtue, or they think they don't need it. Beware this group. They have breakdowns on everybody else's time. They are hardworking, intense, somber people who do no foolishness in life and abide none in anyone else. Working with them is like sitting on sandpaper. It doesn't kill, but it's never comfortable. They need some softening along the edges, some marshmallow in their veins. Mark Twain had this category in mind, I think, when asked where he wanted to spend eternity. "Heaven for the climate," he said, "and hell for the company." Sober saints can drive the world to sin.

There are obstacles to laughter, however, that pass as virtues in the people who possess them. One is negative spirituality, an acerbic approach to life in the name of righteousness. These people are the dangerous kind. Not only do they intimidate small children in church, but they pass judgment on good parties as well. They make themselves harbingers of the God of Wrath. These types brook no nonsense in the pursuit of holiness. These types make holiness a plague rather than a passion.

Sometimes, in the interests of sanctity, they call humor Levity—note the capital L. Sometimes, depending on how classical they're feeling at the moment, they call it buffoonery. It all comes down to the same thing as far as they're concerned: empty-headedness. These people take as their truth that laughter diminishes the sacredness of life. Qoheleth and I (and God, too, if we take the Bible in earnest) think otherwise. It is our somber assessment that it is laughter that makes the seriousness of life bearable, makes it transparent, makes it to size. Sarah laughed, God laughed, and the Book of Proverbs laughs. That is pretty important laughing.

The second obstacle to the presence of laughter in life comes from preoccupation with perfectionism. "Imagination," Horace Walpole wrote, "was given to us to compensate us for what we are not. A sense of humor was provided to console us for what we are." The need to surpass ourselves drains every ounce of energy from the human psyche. Nothing funny, nothing fun, can seep into the soul of a person on the way to pseudo-perfection. These are brittle types who cannot afford to take anything lightly for fear they find themselves more human than marble. These people play Bach, never chopsticks. They dance the Tango, never the Chicken.

These people have forgotten, if they ever knew, that there are some things that must always be laughed at in life:

1. Laugh when people tell a joke. Otherwise you might make them feel bad.

2. Laugh when you look into a mirror. Otherwise you might feel bad.

3. Laugh when you make a mistake. If you don't, you're liable to forget how ultimately unimportant the whole thing really is, whatever it is.

4. Laugh with small children. It will restore your delight in the fundamental things of life. It will also improve your sense of humor. Have you ever noticed what children laugh at? They laugh at mashed bananas on their faces; mud in their hair; a dog nuzzling their ears; the sight of their bottoms as bare as silk. It renews your perspective. Clearly, nothing is as bad as it could be.

5. Laugh at situations that are out of your control. When the best man comes to the altar without the wedding ring, laugh. When the dog jumps through the window screen at the dinner guests on your doorstep, sit down and laugh awhile. When you find yourself in public wearing mismatched shoes, laugh—as loudly as you can. Why collapse in mortal agony? There's nothing you can do to change things now. Besides, it is funny. Ask me; I've done it.

6. Laugh at anything pompous, at anything that needs to puff its way through life in robes and titles. Laugh at female-females and the chauvinistic men whose fraudulent philosophy of sex created them. It will free you from their power and give them back their limited place in the universe. More than that, because laughter is a social virtue, it will help the rest of us see the difference between what is authentic in life and what is not. Will Rogers laughed at all the public institutions of modern life. For instance, "You can't say civilization isn't advancing," he wrote. "In every war they kill you in a new way." And thanks to

his laughter we began to see what was going on around us in fresh and shocking perspective.

7. Finally, laugh when all your carefully laid plans get changed: when the plane is late and the restaurant is closed and the last day's screening of the movie of the year was yesterday. You're free now to do something else, to be spontaneous for a change, to take a piece of life and treat it with outrageous abandon.

There are some things, of course, that do not qualify for laughter, that do not refresh the human heart, that set out to hurt whole classes of people, in fact, and that should never, under any conditions, be tolerated under the pretense of humor. Ridicule passed off as wit only reinforces determining stereotypes that justify the ongoing oppression of a people. More to the point, it measures the stature of those who stoop to it. Johann Wolfgang von Goethe wrote, "People show their character in nothing more clearly than by what they think laughable." Ethnic jokes and sexist sneers and racial slurs and jeering at physical limitations do not empty the human soul of debris. They simply fill it with a venom disguised as humor.

The sign of laughter gone sour lies clearly in the charge, "What's the matter with her? Can't she take a joke?" Then the laughter goes hollow or guttural, weak or low. Though nothing at all may be said, everyone knows on the spot that kindness and clear vision have flown the place forever. Then humor itself becomes an instrument of oppression. It gets more difficult at a moment like that to look into the face of the people who have borne the brunt of a tacky laugh and say, "I love you." "Laughter," Charlie Chaplin wrote, "is the tonic, the relief, the surcease for pain." Laughter, that response of the gods to the wonderful foolishness of life, should never cause the kind of ache that makes a person embarrassed to be alive.

In the final analysis, we should laugh at anything that is not a matter of life and death. The trick is to remember that only life and death are life and death. Then the canvas is broad and the palette is deep. The whole world becomes a jester's paradise in which we laugh at what we did not foresee. Who knows? The foibles of time and the shortcomings of life may be God's secret gift of play to us. The psychiatrist Karl Menninger taught that play in life is the only opportunity we ever really have to be free, to make our own decisions, to escape the chains of protocol, the crucifixion of personal projects, and the pressure of social expectations.

The court jester, ancestor of the modern clown and a familiar figure in the Middle Ages, was the symbol of God's Fool, the one who lived by standards "called foolish to many." The court jester reminds us of the spiritual benefits of laughter.

The grace to laugh at ourselves and to chortle at others, where cruel and burdening judgment could otherwise have been, is an antidote against the certification of the God of Vengeance that troubles our weak and flimsy world. If we ourselves, paltry and petty as we are, do not grind faults into the necks of those around us, neither, the theology of humor implies, shall a munificent and loving God.

Laughter is the atrium to wisdom. "Never try to teach a pig to sing," the Sufi say. "It only frustrates the teacher and irritates the pig." Life will never be flawless, but laughter makes of the flaws a gratifying and gracious patchwork piece.

Laughter is an antidote to dualism, a necessary foundation of mental health. To the one who laughs, life is good, the world is good, goodness is the ground on which we walk. No dualism here, no fear of body or soul, no rejection of the tattered truth of our existence. Just gentle, gentle wholeness tenderly handled, lovingly held.

Finally, laughter enables us to live in a highly structured world without falling prey to the manacles of the mind that blind our eyes and cement our hearts. Laughter gives us the freedom of the Jesus who foolishly questioned the authority of the state and smilingly stretched the imagination of the church. "The poor shall inherit the Kingdom," he laughed. "The Kingdom of Heaven is like a woman," he smiled. "God is a daddy," he chuckled. He danced from town to town, healing, making people smile with new hope, bringing invitations to people in trees and light-footedness to lepers. He fished where there were no fish. He invited guests to eat with him when he had no food. He taught babies and poked fun at Pharisees and told winsome little stories, spiritual jokes, about women who would not let pretentious judges alone.

Day after day he smiled his way from one theological absolute to another and left the world with enough to smile about till the end of time.

Once we learn to laugh and play, we will have come closer to understanding our laughing, playing God. The God of ridiculous promises is a God who laughs, a God to be laughed at and laughed with, until that moment when all pain washes away and only the laughter of God is left to be heard in the heavens.

A Time for
War

I have never been able to forget the sight of the mass graves in Russia. They held the bones of twenty million young soldiers who had died in World War II defending the country in their own backyards. In city after city the mounds covered the landscape, raised like huge welts on the national body as far as the eye could see. It was an entire generation of Russian manhood gone. I remember, too, the looks of horror on the faces of the Russian women left behind in that war when they pleaded with our small, pathetically unrenowned delegation, "Peace, please." They have been haunting memories. Most of all, these graves, these faces, have acted as filter for every story of war I have ever read since: Bosnia, Rwanda, Palestine, El Salvador, Nicaragua, Iraq, South Africa, the entire litany of political sin, all the deaths, all the pleas for peace. I came to realize then why it is so difficult to write about war in the United States of America.

The United States of America has waged wars—some of them for great and noble ideals, some for the basest of motives; some to rescue people, some to maintain cheap oil. But whatever the international involvements, the country has never really known war. We have counted our body bags but never lost our old people, our infants, our homes, our cities, the future of our families, our country itself. War has been an exercise in glory for us, a silent worm in the heart of the nation, seducing its character, draining its resources, hardening its heart, becoming its business, undergirding its exports, always enhancing its advancement, never really taxing our security, our economic base, or our predictable future. When I was a grade-school teacher, it was still true to teach children that wheat was the major export of the United States. Now, to teach with integrity, we must admit to this generation that weapons are. Clearly, we traffic in our own demise. We are the gravediggers of the world. Worse, perhaps, we sell death to the highest bidder and call it "security."

"Those who mount a wild elephant go where the wild elephant goes," Randolph Bourne wrote. It is a graphic analogy. We are in a situation of our own making that has run wildly out of control and is taking us with it. What we have disguised as patriotism is clearly a design for genocide. No doubt about it, if we are to save the soul of this country, it is time to make war on war.

Scripture presents us with a clear image of the situation in the story of David and Goliath. Here we do not have a picture of armies ranged on the plains in bold array, sterling in their ideals, virtuous in their motives. No, the vignette does not depict a war between political enemies; it depicts the war between the innocent idealist and the professional enemy. The young David is not at war with warriors; David is at war with an idea that only coincidentally happens to be a person. Goliath is the depersonalized opposition; David the innocent noncombatant, the innocent victim. Neither has an army at his side; neither, in defeating the other, can really defeat the whole machine of war that lies somewhere outside the frame lurking in wait to war again.

"There are a thousand hacking at the branches of evil to every one who is striking at the root," Thoreau wrote. We cannot, in other words, eliminate war by warring. That is simply striking at its branches, an exercise in the survival of the fittest, perhaps, but not necessarily a guarantee of the survival of the best. No, we can eliminate war only by going to the root of the system that makes it possible. We can wage war on war only by eliminating the violence in our own hearts that makes war acceptable, patrician, glorious: "For God and Country," "For the Fatherland," "For the Flag."

War is a depredation of the human spirit that is sold as the loftiest of livelihoods. To hide the rape and pillage, the degradation and disaster, the training of human beings to become animals in ways we would allow no animals to be, we have concocted a language of mystification. We count casualties now in terms of "collateral damage," the number of millions of civilians we are prepared to lose in nuclear war and still call ourselves winners. We call the deadliest weapons in the history of humankind the most benign of names: Little Boy, Bambi, Peacekeepers. The nuclear submarine used to launch Cruise missiles that can target and destroy 250 first-class cities at one time, for instance, we name *Corpus Christi*, Body of Christ, a blasphemy used to describe the weapon that will break the Body of Christ beyond repair. We take smooth-faced young men out of their mothers' kitchens to teach them how to march blindly into death, how to destroy what they do not know, how to hate what they have not seen. We make victims of the victors themselves. We call the psychological maiming, the physical squandering, the spiritual distortion of the nation's most vulnerable defenders "defense." We turn their parents and sweethearts and children into the aged, the widowed, and the orphaned before their time. "We make a wasteland and call it peace," the Roman poet Seneca wrote with miserable insight.

The scene is burned into my mind to this very day. At the foot of the casket of my twenty-year-old cousin, an only child, killed in Vietnam just weeks before his military discharge, my gentle uncle recited again and again for all to hear his one consolation: his good boy, he said, "had at least died a hero." I thought of the burning villages and displaced children and raped girls and defenseless dead farmers left behind in other graves in another place that day and, with nothing heroic in sight, went silent and looked away. I knew that young soldiers were victims too.

But "what if someone gave a war and no one came?" Carl Sandburg asked. What if a government tried to wage war but the people said no? Imagine it. What if mothers would not give their sons to the slaughter and their daughters to the kill? What if fathers would not train their children to the obedience of robots and the obscenity of machoism? What if the churches really began to preach what they say they endorse and prepared their young people in conscientious objection as well as in the catechism? What if we did not count the death of 150,000 Iraqi children under the age of five a thing to boast about as victory? What if pastors refused to ring church bells to celebrate the massacre of the masses? What if military chaplains were expected to be as clear about their objection to nuclear weapons as they are to their rejection of abortion? What if we quit kidding ourselves that war was any longer a military thing and faced the fact that it is now more a pogrom of innocents? Both theirs and ours.

What if we took nonviolent resistance seriously? What if we not only refused to cooperate with enemies but also refused to become like them in murderous ways. "The sword which we use to kill our enemy," Augustine taught, "must pass first through our own hearts." Clearly, the things we have devised to kill the others are killing us as well. They are killing our schools; they are ruining our infrastructure; they are destroying our social services; they are wringing our souls inside out.

We have become, indeed, a nation at war with itself. The blood of our own children runs in our streets because we have taught them violence well. The best armed nation in the world is the least safe. The melting pot has become a cauldron of tensions.

The question for our time, then, has become a basic question of human nature: What exactly will it take to rid the giant of violence in us? Are we doomed to devise our own destruction? Can we outlive the technological monsters we have created? And if so, how? "The next world war will be fought with stones," Einstein warned. And he should know.

But there are obstacles to the elimination of war so insidious that good people refuse to believe they exist. There is a colossus in our own soul more dangerous than the titan we imagine outside ourselves that cries to be tamed before we shall ever really know peace.

The real public enemies of our time are power and profit. Both seep into the soul at every level of the national psyche and sicken it to the core. The profit motive seduces the entire country in subtle, ingratiating ways. When the economy is good, for instance, no one who lives off the military money that the war machine generates questions how it got that way. The fact that people take prostitution wages to work in plants that prepare the death of the globe masks itself under the great conspiracy of silence and calls itself "a leading economic indicator." No one protests the fact that we will borrow money for war but we will not borrow it for education or job training or subsidized housing. "We'll miss the security of the bases," a farmer in one region said to the interviewer when they began dismantling the missile launchers that marked his cornfield Ground Zero in a rural Kansas territory. And he never even blinked when he said it.

We have learned to call a recipe for global destruction good. We have come to think of a military industrial economy that enslaves us to war as freedom. We have accepted the fact that the greatest military volatility that the world has ever known is security. We have come to call up, down; wrong, right; and national madness, sanity.

Once upon a time, an ancient story tells, the main tributary of a mountain stream became polluted. Everyone in the village became crazed with the exception of those few people who refused to drink the water. Finally, ridiculed for their differences, sick to death from loneliness, and facing dried-up wells, those who refused to drink from the stream went to the king to ask what they should do in such a dire situation.

And the wise old king said, "It is clearly madness to drink this water, but if drink it we must, let us at least have the honor of sending out messengers to tell the rest of the world that we know that we are mad."

Clearly, evil has seeped into the soul of the nation but calls itself good, calls itself "freedom," calls itself "defense." And that may be the greatest madness of all. If we could only know the enormity of our spiritual distortion perhaps we could be cured of it. "I never wonder to see men wicked," Jonathan Swift wrote, "but I often wonder to see them not ashamed." We need, indeed, to expunge the leviathan within us that has robbed us of our shame. We need to become human again. We need to see that what has led us to our profits and pretended to moral power has really led us to our peril.

There is a second national nemesis that plagues us as well. The military economy is not our only civic pitfall. We have as well the moral disease of domination, with which we must struggle for our souls. Power has become our national obsession, as it has for so many nations before us and around us. Like countries we say we are not like, we traffic in death and dirty deals, in guerrilla warfare against the innocent and rape of the resources for the military. Clearly, we are not alone in the love of power, nor in our acceptance of whatever it takes to get it.

We, too, whatever our talk of freedom, have fallen prey to the disease of domination. "America must lead," the politicians say, and they mean, it seems, that the United States must broker the morals of the world. Except we don't. And we can't. Not this way, at least. We talk human rights and then ignore it anyplace that has no oil. We are powerless in Bosnia with all our weapons; we are hijacked in Haiti despite our bombers; we are totally disarmed in Rwanda—if we even care enough about Rwanda to notice—despite our bombs. We have bartered moral suasion for brute force. We have left ourselves with the unanswered question of exactly what can be valuable enough to unleash upon the world the hoary promise of its extinction.

But why is it like this? Why? Answers suggest themselves but only with a blush: Is it because of some small dark thing niggling at our starving souls? Is it because we have come to some state of spiritual bankruptcy? Is it because, even as churches, we have given more energy to our institutions, perhaps, than we have to the gospel? Is it because we have spent more time saying our prayers to get into heaven than we have listening to the prophets who warn us that the reign of God must start first on earth if it is ever to start for us at all? Yes, of course. For all these reasons. But not only.

The fact is that we cling to the image of the Warrior God in the face of the God of Love.

The fact is that we mix the national religion and the Christian religion as a matter of course. This country, we presume, like the Jerusalemites before us, is especially favored by God, under God's singular protection, distinctly chosen to do God's will. To those types Abraham Lincoln taught in the course of the Civil War, "The question is not whether or not God is on our side. The question is whether or not we are on God's side."

We abhor violence but we do not, as a people or a church, study nonviolence. We abhor conflict but we do not demand national research in alternative methods of conflict resolution. We are often besieged by noble frustration in the face of historical injustice and, frustrated by our powerlessness, choose to send our young people into international conflict rather than participate in public resistance activities ourselves in their behalf.

We are just as often stricken with a fear of sharing that closes our borders and ignores the unacceptable of the world and deports the economically defenseless.

As a result, our enemies and their hidden armies are alive and well, we are powerless in the face of international evil, and militarism in our society reigns supreme while people starve to death because we have refused to be a welfare state and chosen to be a warfare state instead.

It is time for us to withdraw our support for war as we once withdrew it from the bartering for women, the institution of slavery, and the practice of chaining the mentally ill. War is a barbarian approach to contemporary problems. It is madness raised to high art. It is technological insanity. It does not work anymore, unless, of course, the wholesale slaughter of men, women, and children is called peace.

The spiritual effect of rejecting war as a way to resolve human tension is to become a person of peace, too strong to be intimidated even by our own, too involved to be silenced while the arms dealers sell weapons that only make bad situations worse, too human to be turned into a death machine. The function of the peacemaker is not to shirk combat with evil. The function of the peacemaker is to find ways to confront evil without becoming evil.

It is not that a peacemaker is not willing to die for something. It is simply that a peacemaker is not willing to kill for it.

The truth is that there is no such thing as a necessary war. "Violence does even justice unjustly," Thomas Carlyle teaches. There is no vindication in violence. If war comes it is because our vision has shriveled, our spirits have gone sour, our hearts have lost the way. But if that is the case, then our future is in far more jeopardy than we know.

"The saints of our time," Camus wrote, "are those who refuse to be either its executioners or its victims." We must, in other words, stop feeding the innocent to the brutally barbaric in the name of high ideals. The child with the puny slingshot who breathes in the center of each one of us knows that, though we may well be destroyed if we go without military might into the fray, being armed to the hilt is no guarantee of victory either. It is time for a commitment to nonviolent resistance. If war we must, let it be with the brutality, the degradation, and the violence within ourselves. That will certainly be the only thing that in the end can possibly save us from ourselves.

A Time to
Heal

I remember the rush of insight that seeped through me the day
I realized the situation. It had suddenly occurred to me that
none of us can really be sure that we understand the Book of
Ecclesiastes. What's more, I realized that maybe no one is supposed to be able to grasp its meanings completely, in one burst of
consciousness, in one gift of light. Maybe it is supposed to come
over us slowly, in layers, one bright moment at a time when life
becomes new with pain, fresh with joy, different from its begin-
nings. Maybe it is the very obscurity of the Book of Ecclesiastes
that is its meaning.

The problem with the book lies in the fact that it is very de-
ceptive. It reads with such simplicity that, at first glance, it stands
there disarmingly transparent, almost simplistic—"a time for this,
a time for that," it insists—monotonous and droning, hypnotic and
obvious, and, apparently, of not much use. Unless, of course, you
think a little. For instance, I realized as I began to struggle with
the themes in it that what was actually being said by the statement

about "a time to heal" was not one message but two. At the first level, its clear sense is not only that there is a time in every life for a person to care about the sufferings of other people, but that there is some obligation to abate them. On the other hand, it is equally clear that the dictum could also mean that there's a period of time in every human life when the process of being healed, of coming beyond my own woundedness, may itself be life's greatest project.

Isn't the implication, then, that personal healing, the cauterization of personal wounds, is part of the natural rhythm of life? That we all need it on every level? That we must all go through it someday or run the risk, ironically, of never being whole because we have never known what it is to be wounded but then healed, to be struck down but still survive? Suffering, after all, is surely not for its own sake.

The thought becomes a haunting challenge. What is it to be beaten by life to the point of death? What is really the role of the good Samaritans of the world? Most of all, how do we come to healing once we've been battered beyond any energy for it? And, finally, who of those figures am I myself at this point in my life— the healer or the one in need of healing? And if I am the one in need of healing, what is my own role in it?

"Calamity is the human's true touchstone," Beaumont wrote. Calamity, in other words, lets loose the fire that tries the gold, the wind that tests the tree, the water that sweeps away everything in life that is not anchored, not grounded, not imbedded in the firmament of our souls. Without calamity what shall we ever be and how shall we ever know it? "I survived the San Francisco earthquake," the T-shirts said. What I had once regarded as a cruel joke, I began to see as a statement of theology, a fierce proclamation of the spirit, rather than the flip response of a culture so unaccustomed to disaster that mockery substitutes for respect.

There is, indeed, a time to heal, important to the healthy, essential to the strong, waiting its moment in each of us.

Healing eludes us, however, at every level of the personal and the political spectrum. People die and leave us aching. Old hurts still sear. Around us, like ghosts stalking in the night, our world erupts in tiny sores of violence and brutality while we watch helpless on television screens in every pub and waiting room in the land. Inside ourselves we feel the pain; outside ourselves we wear a calloused look. We have learned to yawn our way through suffering in volumes unimaginable to generations before us. Healing has become the art of political deals and military violence masking as righteousness on the public level or showing as anger and distance on the personal level. What we cannot resolve we repress. What we cannot control we constrain. But we do not heal. Too often, the pain remains embedded in the human psyche, raw and inflamed, waiting only to vent itself again. We build our defenses, personal and public, higher and higher, always on the ready for the next chance to attack, to take vengeance on those who were vengeful toward us, to hurt what we cannot control. Indeed we do not heal; we simply contain the diseases of the soul under thin veneers of pious virtue as we lie in wait.

One of the most health-conscious cultures on earth, we spend huge sums of money on physical well-being all the time being battered in soul. In a society driven by immensely unhealthy motives of achievement and power, profit and personal acceptance, we find ourselves so bent on winning we are surely doomed to fail. We run faster every day and accomplish less despite it. Worse, perhaps, when we have ground ourselves to the psychological pulp that follows competition and precedes loneliness or rejection or the isolating consequences of success, we sit down in the midst of the pain around us and quit. We lose friends and lose energy and lose hope. We lose the family or the race or the security we had taken for granted. We find in its place a cold, stiff copy of the life we once knew, full of hurt and rupture, tormented by an acrid soul and a bruised heart. The work fails, the relationship ends, the future clouds, the sand shifts. We come to the point where we would rather die inside than try again to reshape what would not bend.

The question is, why? Why do we hold pain to the breast like a fox under a toga that eats our insides out even as we smile. "I'm fine," we say when we do not mean it. "Nothing's wrong," we say when we seethe with hurt. "That's life," we snap when life has struck so hard we would prefer no life at all. "Just ignore it," we say when hurt drives out joy, stampedes trust, consumes our hearts, and saps our every thought.

Then, because we have not attended to the wounds in ourselves, we have no capacity for the pain of others. Because we ourselves have too often refused to heal, we cannot heal others. It is a fearsome carousel, this anesthetizing of the human soul. It jades and blocks and makes us paranoid. It cools us and distances us and leaves us hard of heart. Those who swallow stones, we learn, become stones.

Indeed there is "a time to heal." But how? Healing depends on our own resolve to go out of our way to do what we would not, in any circumstances, choose to do. Healing requires that we reach out, not necessarily to those who have hurt us, but at least to something that gives us new life, new hope, new pleasure. Healing is the process of refusing to be wounded.

The parable of the good Samaritan is not about the curing of one person; it is about the healing of two, both of whom carry the scars of abuse, both of whom reside in us in tandem at all times. One has been beaten in body; the other in soul. One has been wounded by the brutality of people; the other has been wounded by ideas that cripple and limit, that bind a person to small, small worlds and smother the air we breathe. The Samaritan, the outcast, has been wounded and overlooked by society. The Levite, the professional religious of the Establishment culture, has been taught to ignore the wounds of those who do not meet with public approval and so, made close-minded and socially limited, is wounded too. One posture teaches us fear; the other perspective teaches us hate. Whatever the situation, the end result is pain. The question is, how shall either of the battered learn to live again?

Who has not known what it is to be hurt by either hate or neglect, to be passed by on the road of life by those from whom we thought we could certainly expect help? Who has not known what it is to be targeted for scorn or rejection or jealousy or misinterpretation? Who has not felt the stultifying effects of ideas that make us captive to the agendas and ambitions of others and leave us as much oppressed as oppressor? What is the process, then, of coming to wholeness again, once the bonds of human community have been broken? What repairs the breaking of a golden cord? You see, the fact is that enemies can damage us, but they cannot hurt us. Only people we love can do that by what they withhold from us that could give us life, by the lies they teach us that nail our feet to the ground.

There are two obstacles to being healed. The first lies in our attachment to the pain. We cannot heal ourselves of the pains to which we cling. We have to want to be healed. We cannot wear injustice like a red badge of courage and hope to rise from it. Even before we are vindicated, even before restitution comes—if it ever comes—we ourselves must move beyond it, outside of it, despite it.

Healing depends on our wanting to be well. I may not forget

the blows I have suffered in life, but I must not choose to live under their power forever. Most of all, I must not choose to imprison myself in my own pain. Whatever has mutilated us—the betrayal, the dishonesty, the mockery, the broken promises—there is more to life than that. The first step of healing, then, is to find new joy for myself to tide me through the terror of the abandonment. It is time to get a life instead of mourning one. When the beating is over, there is nothing to do but to get up and go on, in a different direction to be sure, but on, definitely on.

The second step in healing is to find new ideas in which to live. Whatever we needed before the breakpoint came—security, love, connectedness, certainty, identity—we must now find someplace else. We must put our hope in risk and find it challenging, in self and find it strong, in newness and find it enough.

The third step to healing is to trust ourselves to someone else just when we think we cannot trust anyone or anything at all. Just when we are not sure who the enemy really is, we must risk confidence in someone again. It is a false and hollow cure that ends with a sterile handshake. Healing comes for both the beaten and the intellectually bound when they step across the lines in their minds and hope that this time, in this person, in this situation, they will find the acceptance, the enlightenment, needed to join the human community one more time.

Healing comes when I have been able to desensitize myself to the indignity of hurt by telling it to death until I have bored even myself with the story. For this I need the Samaritans, the healers, who by taking me into the arms of the heart to let me cry transcend their own small lives and learn about the human condition what they themselves would never have come to, perhaps, without me. We need the Samaritan who listens and understands. It is not the wounding that kills; it is lack of understanding that paralyzes the soul. It is, after all, understanding that every soul on earth is seeking.

The final step in healing is a matter of time itself. To honor the fact that there is "a time for healing" means surely that we come to peace with the notion that healing does not come before its time, that healing takes time, that time itself is a healer who comes slowly, bringing new life and new wisdom in its wake.

The spiritual advantages of healing are obvious for the healer. Healers come to new levels of compassion. Once able to be important in someone else's life, healers come to a new sense of their own personal value. Those who bind the emotional wounds of others find new meaning in life and new love for the unknown other. Those who touch the bleeding soul of another to shape it into new confidence and fresh hope are themselves flooded with a sense of compassionate power. The spiritual advantages of the healing process in healers too are often overlooked. We assume that healing is gratuitous condescension rather than a spiritual discipline of immense proportion and great reward.

Most of all, however, it is the spiritual power of the healing process in each of us that goes unnoted and so unappreciated. We flee the hurts—ignore them and dismiss them and detest them— and so miss the values of the healing time itself. "Where there is sorrow, there is holy ground," Wilde teaches. It is in the healing process that we come to a new appreciation of life. What the human being survives is the mark of the mettle of humanity. What we manage to transcend is what we have triumphed over. What we have wrestled with and won is what measures in us the quality of our lives.

The Samaritan, by reaching out and touching the pain of another, throws her own life open to new significance. The wounded who walk away from their pain into unknown and unsought ways instead of spending life awash in it show all of us that life upon life awaits those whose minds are made up to live, whatever the beatings, whatever the traps, whatever the muggings along the way. "Pain is life," Charles Lamb wrote. "The sharper the pain, the more evidence of life." Pain, we learn as life goes on, is simply one more entrance into life, one more challenge to change things.

A Time to
Sow

The philosopher Arthur Schopenhauer made an observation that for all intents and purposes has become the theme of the modern world. "Change alone," he wrote, "is eternal, perpetual, immortal." And sure enough, in an age driven by computer technology, global communications, and interplanetary exploration, change has become the modern mantra of a fast-paced world. It pulses under the culture like an artery in spasm. Change propels our daily decisions beyond old concerns for quality to new pre-occupations with improvement. We don't buy furniture to last a lifetime anymore; we buy with an eye to remodeling it or adapting it or to maintaining its resale value.

The thought of constant change colors our sense of the future. We wear it like a logo as we race from experience to experience, from place to place, and now, in our time, from idea to idea, from concept to concept, from social revolution to social revolution.

A culture that once took equilibrium for certain now takes change for granted. We may, in fact, take it far too much for granted.

Change, after all, is not a given. Change follows in the wake of something that preceded it, quiet as a shift in wind. It does not just happen; it is not a timed process. "If we're just patient; if we just wait long enough, it has to come," we say when we do not want to be responsible ourselves for the change. But change does not just come; change is brought somehow.

Change comes with the coming of critical mass, with the unrelenting build-up of circumstances until the circumstances themselves cry to heaven for attention.

Wanting the end of slavery did not bring it. People who were willing to die for freedom brought it. Waiting for the fall of monarchy did not assure it. Thinkers who spent their lives exploring the philosophy of human institutions planted the seeds that led to its downfall and made other systems possible. Desegregation did not just come. Martin Luther King marched thousands of people through the cities of this nation to get it. Suffrage for women did not just come. Grandmothers went to jail to get it. Vietnam did not just end. Young people left the country or took to the streets in droves to stop it. The Berlin Wall did not just fall. People dismantled it. The Polish Communist government did not just decide to negotiate with the citizenry after years of authoritarianism. Thousands of workers formed Solidarity, the trade union that brought down a brutal state. "Time changes nothing," the proverb teaches. "People do."

Depending on time to provide a life free of anguish and full of opportunity for beaten women and poor children does not create it. Women and men who expose themselves to derision and ridicule, thanks to their work for equality and liberation, provide the impulse that makes for social change. Peace does not come by preparing for war. Peace comes because people din our hearts with the raw truth of our own participation in human brutality.

They march in public and spend long years in jail on our behalf until finally they manage to drag us back from the brink of our warring hearts by standing there, the fire of conscience in our frozen souls.

No, wanting the perfect job, the loving family, a just society, the balanced life, a renewed church does not guarantee the good life, the new world, the revolution, the Jesus life. Change, real change, the kind of change that touches the soul as well as the environment, is not instantaneous. It is slow and labored and painful. It does not come easily; it exacts a price; it demands a dull commitment. Ecclesiastes in its commitment to the singular process of preparedness is very clear about that.

Life, Ecclesiastes leads us to understand, is not about change; life is about sowing. And therein lie both the struggle and the gift. The function of each succeeding generation is not to demand change; it is to prepare for it. The function of one generation is to make change possible for the next. The real function of each generation is to sow the seeds that will make a better world possible in the future. "Let us plant dates even though those who plant them will never eat them," Rubem Alves wrote. "We must live by the love of what we will never see. . . . Such disciplined love is what has given prophets, revolutionaries, and saints the courage to die for the future they envisaged. They make their own bodies the seed of their highest hope." Even in the face of the impossible, we must act as if the miracle will come tomorrow. That's what sowing is all about. It requires trying when hope is thin and faith is stretched and opposition is keen.

An Arab proverb teaches: "Every morning I turn my face to the wind and scatter my seed. It is not difficult to scatter seeds but it takes courage to go on facing the wind." The ability to stand steadfast in the face of opposition is the real charism of the sower. The commitment to say a different truth in the face of those who call you liar is the virtue of the sower. The willingness to sow seed on barren ground, on rock, and in thorn bushes is the prophetic task of the sower. Today, for instance, the American people lament the state of the American school system and the lack of health care programs and the loss of employment opportunities as one form of economic development yields to another. Yesterday, however, they said nothing about the amount of money that went into militarism. Yesterday countless numbers of men wanted to advance in the company and double their salaries. Today their children are gone from home before they ever got to know their fathers, and there is little left on which to spend all the extra money they finally earned. Today too many women still bemoan the loss of half their lives but for a thousand yesterdays spent themselves being pleasers and helpers, dependents who, living vicariously, never learned to live at all. What the world really needed through all these periods were people who were willing to cry out forever unheard, if necessary, until the world had ears to hear. Clearly, what we want for tomorrow we will have to begin doing today. That is what sowing is all about.

Sowing, however, is a tedious task whose enemy is the need to succeed. It took thousands of years, for instance, to eliminate slavery—and hundreds of them were spent here in "the land of the free, the home of the brave," where people could not, would not, see that the humans in front of them were really human. Governments legislated for slavery; businesses depended on it; churches theologized it. And generation upon generation upon generation who wanted to be loyal to the government, successful in business, pious in their churches went along with the thinking, went along with the sin of sacramentalized slavery when, with half a teaspoon of a sower's courage, they could have been planting new questions in the human soul.

Nor has the situation changed much. We are only now beginning to doubt the morality and inevitability of nuclear war. The idea of the genuine equality of women is embarrassingly recent—and in too many places has yet to be accepted. Indeed, it is a world in need of sowing.

There are obstacles to sowing, though. Sowing taxes the energy of the soul. Sowing takes a long, long time. Those who sow must be prepared never to see the result of their work. Results they must leave to a generation of harvesters. For now there is only the long, tiresome chore of starting small seeds in dark ground and waiting to see what, if anything, grows. The process is a long and empty one. No bands blare for the solitary sower. No festivals celebrate the process of imagining.

Tedium exhausts the person of ideas. Telling and retelling the idea to hostile audiences and skeptical friends and outraged neighbors and traditionalist congregations and heartsick families takes its toll on the spirit. "What's the use . . . Eat, drink, and be merry" is the temptation that comes too often, too easily to those whose lot in life is to sow on arid ground.

The spirituality of the sower, then, is the spirituality of urgent patience. They demand for now what others do not even know is lacking. People listen but do not believe or people do not listen at all. People listen and scoff. People listen and argue. People listen and yawn. People listen and reason the unreasonable. It is too painfully true: the business of changing the world one heart at a time requires the courage of the mountain climber who goes alone where none have been to plant the flag of the human possibility that no one sought.

It is not an easy thing, this sowing the seeds of the next human frontier, the next layer of moral imagination in the always unfinished and frustratingly ongoing process of creation. Those who need to know success need not apply. Sowing is for people of conscience only, for people who cannot live with themselves if they live on a lesser level than they know in their hearts life is really meant to be. They deal with ridicule; they feel rejection; they know the dailiness of defeat.

Sowers must believe in the "fullness of time." "Jesus came," the Evangelist explains, "when all things were in the fullness of time." When everything was ready. When the confluence of consciousness, need, possibility, and charismatic personalities were all in place, were all at the moment of precious perfection. When the ground was good and the field was tilled and the water was abundant and the process was right. The problem for the sower is that there is no way whatsoever to know with certainty exactly when that will ever be.

"How many snowflakes does it take to break a branch?" the snowbird asked.

"No one knows," the storm cloud answered.

"My job is simply to keep on snowing until it does."

"Ah, yes," said the snowbird sadly, "and who knows how many voices will be needed to bring peace?"

The role of the sower is simply to build up the fullness of time, to work without ceasing, never knowing when the seed will root, never quitting until it does. The sower sows even when the sowing seems in vain so that no moment is lacking in the preparation, so that not doing something does not become just as much an obstruction to the coming of the new creation as doing something contrary would be.

No doubt about it, sowing is a slow and arduous process that has all the power it takes to harden the hearts and break the spirits of those for whom desire is demand and possibility is expectation. In a culture of instantaneous results, sowing is an act of high discipline.

But sowing has its own spiritual fruits. Trust flames from a sower's heart, like sparks on an anvil. The sower lives by the light of what cannot be seen and may never come, but the sower does not desist. With a dogged devotion to the desirable but undetermined, sowers go through life sure of a God who wants better for us.

Abandonment becomes the sower's art. Life lived at the edge of the almost-but-not-really periods in life demands that we throw ourselves on an unfinished tomorrow with all the energy we have. Planting ideas and questions and possibilities in the human psyche, like planting the fields of the desert, is at best a desolate and potentially devastating moral duty. After all, the sowers may never know whether their lives really had any value at all. "If you expect to see the results of your work," the Talmud teaches, "you have simply not asked a big enough question."

Trust and abandonment mark the souls of the sowers, true. But something even more profound, perhaps, marks their lives. Sowers know conviction and know purpose in proportions largely unknown to the complacent and the uncomprehending of the world who go through life satisfied with their present and uncaring of someone else's future. It takes a focused soul to want something badly enough in the future to give all of life to preparing for it now, too often alone, too frequently ignored.

Ice-cold certitude of soul attends the sower's sanctification process. To the sowers, the goal is more compelling than its obstacles. Steady, steady presence is the color of their lives. Sowing requires the art of vision, the science of conviction. "I would rather fail in a cause I know must someday triumph," Wilkie wrote, "than succeed in a cause I know must someday fail."

The spiritual life of the sower is plagued by discouragement and failure, yes, but tinged as well by wide-eyed hope and unflappable certainty. Sowers envisioned the end of slavery and equal roles for women, for instance, before most people even saw the evils. They see a vision and are blinded by it. They fail and fail and fail only to try again.

Sowers live in the mind of God and know with surety that what is not good for everyone in the Garden is not the will of God. They stand immersed in a consciousness of the essential frailty of the human condition but committed nevertheless to the divine dream for humankind, knowing that if God wills it, then human beings are capable of it.

For the seeker with the soul of a sower, the time to sow is now. Always now. Whatever the future. However long before "the fullness of time."

A Time to
Die

It is a truly terrible question, of course, but, in the long run,
may be one of the few questions in life that are really worth
asking. The basic inquiry of the human condition deceives.
"What is there that is worth living for?" we ask, when the essential question of the human enterprise may more truly be,
"What is the value of a life that lives devoid of anything worth
dying for?" Allan Boesak wrote from the center of the seething
struggle against apartheid in South Africa, "We will go before
God to be judged and God will ask, 'Where are your wounds?
. . . Was there nothing worth dying for?'" And the Cuban poet
José Marti wrote, "When others are weeping blood, what right
have I to weep tears?" The question is, is life to be hoarded for
the sake of a private existence that is safe and secure, or is it to be
gambled recklessly away on the chance of becoming more than
a standard-brand human being with a standard-brand character? What is really worth the expenditure of a life? The answers
plague and provoke us. One false step and we doom ourselves to

the level of human cutouts, to a Ken and Barbie Doll existence that dulls the soul to tears.

The variety of responses to these questions of human turmoil are legion and ageless and paltry. Often very, very paltry indeed. For some, the preservation of the Roman empire was good enough motive to lay down their lives. For some, popes and papal states commanded their allegiance and laid claim to their fragile futures. For some it was the Yorks in the War of Roses that merited their lives. For some, Adolf Hitler and his raging dreams of German superiority were enough cause to compel the waste of an entire generation. For some it was Genghis Khan. For some it was Richard Nixon and Vietnam and communism too weak on its feet to survive. For some it has been a thousand dictators, a hundred fleeting political systems, ages upon ages of wars for greed and wars for land and struggles for power. And in the end, all of these fleeting causes are barely remembered now or lost sway ages ago, each of them miserable mistakes of the human spirit, each of them supplanted by another overrated hero, another empty tyrant. Each of them, in the long view of history, pales and fades and fails to jog memories, let alone command hearts. Few of them, if any, seem now to have been worth a single human life, one moment of support. No, it is not of plastic contests such as these that Ecclesiastes speaks.

Ecclesiastes conjures up the torrent of circumstances that surround the death of justice and love—unthinking enemies, faithful friends, terrible betrayals, and the enlightenment that can come out of the deepest of darknesses. It confronts death with both questions and answers. The purpose of wanton death is not simply to satisfy the jaws of life with compliant victims. The function of the death of the self is to throw a thousand question marks across the sky that demand to know from us not so much what is worth dying for, but what we consider worth living for.

"The difference between poetry and rhetoric," Audre Lorde writes in her poem "Power," "is being ready to kill yourself instead of your children." The image is a sharp and poignant one. It weighs our souls and measures our quality. It is rhetoric, flat-footed prose, that defines the systems that control us. It is poetry, a vision beyond sight, that elevates us above the mundane, that defies the things of the mind for the things of the spirit. Rhetoric dies to enable and maintain the present, one unthinking act at a time. Poetry dies to enable the future. Being the rhetoricians of society, being unwilling to die if necessary to change society's sick self, means choosing to survive the present social disease ourselves and permitting our children, the next generation, to die from it instead. When we tolerate sexism, for instance, in order to survive it, we condemn our children to its destruction. Abiding nuclearism so that we can profit from it means that we condemn our children to its dangers. Being the poets of society, being willing to give our own lives so that others "may have life and have it more abundantly" is a call to a thousand glorious little deaths.

Rhetoric, Lorde suggests, is used and misused to glorify systems for their own sakes whatever the number of deaths it takes to sustain them. Rhetoric feeds the children of the generation to the distortions of our own desires. "Young men fight old men's wars," the proverb teaches. The poetry of the soul, on the other hand, demands much more than the service of the political self. Poetry commands a far higher impulse than the order of the state. Poetry requires first and foremost a care for the children of our dreams who bear on their backs the burden of our vision—or our lack of it. Poetry feeds the human spirit and so frees the shackles of generations to come. Poetry forces us to face ourselves and die a little so that others may live.

To die to maintain a distorted present is rhetoric; to die for the sake of a more human future for others is poetry.

Tomorrow can triumph only when we put to death in ourselves everything that is not lifegiving today. Human possibility, not politics, is what poetry is about, and because of it generations after us live in the light of a wisdom won by dint of social critique and personal risk. Only if we ourselves have died a little can we confront the synagogues of society, the sanhedrins of our own systems with lepers who are cured beyond the pale of our policies and women who rise from the cemeteries of our social graces.

Henry Van Dyke puts it very clearly, "Some people are so afraid to die that they never begin to live." The dilemma is, of course, that we become so enamored of life at any price that we most stand to lose it just when it seems that we have merited it most. So afraid are we of losing what we have that we temporize with things that bring death and call them life-giving. We waste our most precious human resources on the cult of death, for instance, and call it "defense." We swallow our ethics in board rooms and call it "business." We suppress the development of half the human race and call it "woman's role" for them. We crucify in others what we should be dying to in ourselves. We thrive on racism and sexism and militarism and never say a word because we have never unearthed its effects in ourselves, never brought to light its toxins in ourselves, never let it die in us so that something better could grow there. "The unexamined life is not worth living," Socrates said. But Socrates was wrong. The fact is that the unexamined life is no life at all.

We cower and grovel and crumble before the powers that be in order to be them ourselves and never know the darkness in our hearts. We see the system around us, taste its poison fruits, wallow in its acid, and never name its disease in us. We tolerate every manner of evil the world has ever known and call it good. We call gay bashing "freedom of speech" and the invisibility of women's issues "the Divine Plan" and racism "the natural law" and the nuclearization of the globe "patriotism." We see the laws that maintain the systems and we never ask, "Who said so? And why? And to whose advantage?" We fail to die to the old ideas so that a new world can spring up fresh.

We bring the heart of the politician to our worlds rather than the spirit of the poet-prophet. We sell our souls to systems that promise us promotion and shrivel ourselves into unconscionable dwarfdom as a result. We listen to slander and scandal and let it kill our minds rather than kill the scurrility of the conversations themselves. We go up in the world on the backs of those we have left behind. An immigrant nation, we resist immigration with all our hearts for fear it means less for us as well as enough for them. Women argue that they are not oppressed in order to support men and, in the doing of it, fail to die to the lethal effects of sexism in themselves. We accept systems in church and state alike with never a hint of public skepticism about their goals or products or philosophy, sanctifying them on the momentum of their longevity rather than their fundamental morality. We give ourselves over to death-dealing forces in society and call it life and, as a result, become the death-dealers ourselves. Through it all, we protest our innocence of the rape of the world and perform the hand-washings of our souls.

But Ecclesiastes says that there is "a time to die." What Ecclesiastes does not say is that death is prepared for by little dyings. The fact is that we cannot rise until we are willing to die a little. We can be alive but we cannot be human until we confront the inhuman in ourselves. We cannot bring life until we admit that we are part of the death around us. We cannot give new life until we are ready to scorch and sear and unmask the decadent old slivers of thought and purpose in ourselves. Dying a little, in fact, is what life is all about.

If we are to live well and die for the right things, we must learn to ask, "Who stands with the sufferer, who tortures on behalf of the system and why, who is missing from the scene, and what is the purpose of the dying?" Masochism, in other words, is not a virtue.

Dying is one of life's most difficult processes, however. Its demands sap the soul of all our old rationalizations, all our well-used excuses for saying one thing but doing another, all our pretenses at a goodness that is more social etiquette than social virtue. It cuts us off from the very things that have brought us to the point of where we are. When we begin to die to things in ourselves that once were time-honored and socially acceptable, the danger is, of course, that when the process is over we will no longer even know ourselves. As one set of beliefs gives way to another, new questions rise to haunt us: Whose family are we? Who is our God? Who really are our friends? What is really right? The questions become the scourges of our soul and punish us day and night. We have left the country of ourselves and cannot find our way back into that place again.

Then we find ourselves with weak and powerless friends, toothless creatures who have nothing to give but assurance. We become unsteadied by the unsteadiness of those closest to us who find our questions useless, find our questions mad. "He is a crazy man," his brothers said of Jesus, we remember, when they went to drag him away from the lip of his own unstable ledge of life. Worst of all, perhaps, we face enemies we once called allies. The minions of the system do their duty on us and never, it seems, ask themselves whose duty it is that they do. They salute and take orders. They unleash dogs on the defenseless. They pierce the sides of good people to make sure they cannot rise to speak again. They stumble and falter and flee their associations with us. It is a wearying time, this death of old ideas.

But death does more than snap the bonds of our past and deplete the starch of our souls. Every little death we die turns us into something new and washes us up on the sunlit shore of a different psyche, a person called by the old name but unknown even to ourselves.

Death is resurrection unwanted.

For those who are willing to peel the layers of the mind, to search for ideas that can shape the new even though they do not fit the old, freedom waits. The world begins to spin all over again, and everything is new. No idea is safe from probing; no rule is sacrosanct of its own declaration, no system merits emperor worship. In this world, lepers dance and women think and spittle cures. Anything is possible. God is in charge again. Death becomes life. The tomb becomes a paradise of new perfumes where life lies in wait for those who are willing to begin again.

The spirituality of death, then, is the preserve of those who are willing to look a system in the eye and call it capable of shine, yes, but seriously tarnished nevertheless. "I have not come to destroy the law but to fulfill it," Jesus said of the Tradition that had raised him well enough to be able to see its deficiencies. And they put him to death for the ideas he had already died to in behalf of new life untold times.

"There is a time to die," Ecclesiastes tells us in the face of a Jesus who did, a soldier who did not, and a Peter who spent most of his life avoiding its consequences, as perhaps do we all. There is a time for us to face up to what is over in life and what is decaying in life and what is destructive in life and quit trying to make old ideas fit new situations.

We cling to old ideas and old systems, if for no other reason than because we know them. The price we pay to maintain the impossible is the very development of self, but it is a golden cage we live in, safe and secure and sure in its sense of certain salvation. In this prison, newness is never an option, conformity is a substitute for conviction, ideas are dangerous, and approval is paramount. The Jesus of Nazareth who died convinced that oxen could be taken out of pits on Sabbath days would never be at home here. The Jesus of Nazareth who called those who maintained the letter of the laws better than their spirit "whitened sepulchres" would not be comfortable here. The Jesus of Nazareth who preferred the tomb to the palaces of the privileged would not have brooked such intellectual dishonesty.

There is a spirituality of death that brings light into the shadowland, life into the world, pulse into the flat lines of sickly systems. Without it, the world will never rise again out of its tombs of dry clay into the light of new life. Sachs has said it well, it seems. "Death is more universal than life," he writes. "Everyone dies but not everyone lives."

The spirituality of death is the call to new life in us. What a pity so many avoid it so strenuously, as if the Word of God can possibly know decay.

A Time to
Kill

The ease with which we speak of changing the world, of developing a social conscience, of reshaping ancient patterns of domination, of building a society where "the lion lies down with the lamb" takes everything into account but one. Ourselves. The situation is almost laughable. We set out to change the world and overlook what needs to change in ourselves. We become the standard of what is pure and miss the meaningless of the measure. We completely disregard the seedbed of the profane in the world. The fact is that all the evil of the world resides in the center of the self, in leash if we are lucky, but there nonetheless.

There is no iniquity in life that is not in me in embryo, waiting to get out, struggling to take control of me, worming its way through my life. The little greeds, the small lusts, the puny perfidies, the itchy envies, are all there in my tiny churchgoing heart, if I could only see, if I would only look. One of the necessary degrees of the spiritual life, the sixth-century Rule of Benedict teaches, is to come to realize this, not in neurotic and pious pretension but with every beat of our living hearts. The fact is that there is no base and slimy thing in humankind of which we are not all capable and which we must not come to control before it controls us.

At the same time, true as that may be, the reality is more than it may seem. Life is not simply a series of unending struggles to maintain some kind of cultic purity. Life is a series of learnings as well. St. George the Dragon-killer, the fourteenth-century saint who exemplified for the medieval church the personal problem of confronting evil and overcoming it, and the fifteenth-century mystic Julian of Norwich present a far truer picture of the place of sin in life. The symbol of St. George reminds us that the negotiation of sin is part of every life. Julian and her visions assure us with even more pointedness that "sin is behovable," that sin, in other words, is necessary, that sin is itself an instrument of human development. "God does not punish sin," Julian teaches. "Sin punishes sin."

The truth is a painful one. The seven deadly sins we have called them, these cross-currents of conflict in us, these things that kill the passion for good in the human mind, these things that threaten always to damp the fires of higher purpose in us. Each of them roams restless in our souls, and each of them punishes us with a vengeance that is unremitting. What drives us destroys us.

Greed keeps us in a state of unrelenting tension. We spend our lives grasping for the eternal more until our hearts shrivel from the constancy of wanting.

The unremitting envy of others makes us dissatisfied with all the riches of our own lives. The sight of anything new in anyone else means that suddenly nothing we ourselves have is quite good enough.

Lust makes us incapable of real relationships. People become objects, not friends, not even lovers, just sad excuses of unsustainable comfort.

Pride makes us unaware of the gifting gifts of others. Wrapped up in ourselves we miss what might have come to us through the care and competence of others and so are the poorer for our own limitations all our lives.

Sloth robs us of the joy of personal achievement. Too indolent to try what we know will take great effort, great perseverance, we never know either the cleansing angst of failure or the headiness of success.

Anger stirs the juices of our souls to the point of white heat. We take upon ourselves the righteousness of God and never manage, despite it, to order the universe to our own ends.

Covetousness fills us with turmoil and wearying desire. We cannot possibly enjoy what we have because we are too busy wanting what others have. We lose respect even for ourselves. We are not what others are and we cannot love what we are. Life goes to seed within us.

Indeed, sin is its own punishment. Clearly, all the sin of the world lies burrowed into our own hearts. Obviously there is a time to kill in ourselves whatever it is that is stamping out the spiritual in us, smothering the essential in us.

St. George and the mythical dragon call us to look inside ourselves for the seeds of human bramble, for the detritus of the human condition. No use to look at others, we come to realize. It is time to slay the dragons thrashing about within ourselves, or there is not a single hope that any single life can ignite the world's darkness. Like the tail of a comet, an incomplete sign of what is real but distant, the golden energy for goodness in one of us creates hope in all of us that we too may come to fullness of life before we die. "As you are, so is the world," Ramana Maharshi reminds us. What we cultivate within us we enable around us.

The concept carries immense and disturbing proportion. What sustained slavery was not the slave owners. What sustained slavery were the attitudes in the general public, untested and unacknowledged, that made slavery a given. What sustained slavery were those who never even questioned the unreasonable argument that there were essential differences in the human condition. What sustains huge military budgets outside of wartime is the civilian devotion to enemy making and the refusal of the citizenry to demand from its governments a commitment to the hard work of peace. What maintains the enslavement of women is the almost universal willingness of women to be slaves, to support the governments and husbands and fathers and churches and theology that hold them in their gossamer chains.

St. Pogo says it without nuance: "We have met the enemy and it is us."

Ecclesiastes puts it boldly: "There is a time to kill" the weeds of wickedness within ourselves that enable us to read of rapes and pillage, greed and domination, lies and living holocausts and say not a single word of protest, raise not a single whisper of wonder, give not a single flicker of disgust, raise not a single question of reform. It is time to kill the kind of evil obedience that makes us mindless and marks us with a mentality intellectually subservient enough to make conquerors ecstatic and the conquered weep.

What is it that binds us to our sins? The situation is clear: So immersed are we in the theology of perfectionism that we keep wanting to deny that sin is sin instead of admitting our need to learn from it. When perfectionism is the foundation of spirituality, sin ceases to be functional and error is unacceptable. The only thing to do, then, is to deny our sins and make them virtues. We pay third world peoples slave wages in the name of "development." We wire the world for its total destruction for the sake of "security." We educate and hire and promote and admit into the country only our own kind of people in the interests of "the national good" rather than consider the racism it really is. We exclude whole classes of people from the bounties of church and state and theologize this "eternal plan" for the universe. We make idols out of our systems, high priests out of our officials, and sacrificial lambs out of the ingenuous among us. We do not sin. We justify the corruptions we practice and call them good.

Those who must be perfect, in other words, simply cannot afford to fail. For them, perfection rests in perfection, not in learning how to recover from the struggles that make a human human. A society that is based on perfectionism, then, never says it's sorry, never does penance, never really repents. The perfect simply cling to their perfectionism. It is a sickly condition of the soul.

But perfectionism, the desire to come to a point where we have refined our behaviors enough that we never need to fear relapse, is not the only obstacle to the freedom of spirit that comes with killing the killer-urges to power and things that lie dormant but alive within us. The concept of perfectibility, the idea that anything human can possibly be perfect, constitutes the other great illusion of the spiritual life. It concentrates on the elimination of errors rather than on the value of efforts. If a thing is perfectible, after all, then nothing less than its perfection may really be celebrated. If, on the other hand, a thing is never perfectible, then striving is itself the goal, not the problem. Few people play Mozart's "Minute Waltz" in a minute, but generation after generation tries to conquer the piece and, in the trying, get better and better, happier and happier with themselves.

It is not that sin is not sin. It is simply that sin is not the end of the world—and, in fact, may actually be the beginning of a number of things that can be gained hardly any other way in life and without which life is a pitiful farce. A bout with greed may be precisely what teaches us the freedom of poverty. A struggle with lust may well be what, in the end, teaches us about the real nature of love. A strong dose of anger may be what it takes to teach us the beauty of gentleness.

There are, in other words, things to be learned from sin. One is compassion. Another is understanding. A third is humility. A fourth is perception. Without the ability to own our own sins, these qualities are all hard to come by indeed.

Sin gears us to suffer with those who suffer from the folly of their weaknesses because we have smarted from the folly of our own. Once we can admit our own sins, once we face those things in ourselves that if ever brought to light would be our social downfall, we can companion those for whom the darkness of night has not been so kind. Sin enables us to understand the murderer, to deal justly with the criminal, to control the passion for blood that masks the sins of the righteous with a patina of virtue.

In the end, however, it may be humility and perception that are the best consequences—the intended consequences—of the surfeit of sin. Humility not only identifies us with the human race and confirms the earthiness of the human condition, but it erodes the very basis for hierarchy as well. Humility knows that there are no lords-of-the-manor at all; no one of us at all entitled to subject the rest of us; nobody at all good enough or pure enough to evaluate the rest of us. We are all in struggle. We are all attempting to kill within ourselves the very toxins that poison the human race in general. We are all at the mercy of the God of mercy. We can all learn something from one another.

Unless we can accept our incompleteness, we can never grow from it. Whatever the heights of our present virtue, the bottomless pit of life stretches always before us, always to be catapulted, always to be respected, always in the throes of challenging us to look at ourselves again. Humility reminds us that we are all in process always. More than that, humility reminds us that to be in process is to be perfectly all right, perfectly alive, perfectly human, and perfectly full of life. "It is not where we are that counts," the proverb says. "It is where we are going that matters." And the Chinese teach, "If we stay on the road we are on, we shall surely get where we are going." Humility is the ground for conversion; sin is its seed.

Imagine the perfect person. How dull. What the greatest of saints show us is the greatest amount of triumph, not the greatest amount of bland beauty. Sin and temptation, flawedness and failures are of the essence of life, meant to give us depth, not grounds for despair. What we really need to kill in ourselves is the notion that we have nothing to kill in ourselves at all.

When humility comes, perception comes with it. Then we become capable of seeing that sin and virtue go hand in hand. We can see behind the masks that parade through life as good business acumen and canny politics and fervent religion and incorruptible law. When we begin to understand the undertow in our own soul, we can discover the riptides around us. We can uncover the good in the griminess of business and the saintliness underneath the sinfulness in religion and the great, heaving goodheartedness of most of the world around us. We can see into ourselves and touch tenderly the struggles of the whole, throbbing human race that gropes for fragile virtues and groans in empty-handed dismay. Then we can really learn to love.

There is, indeed, "a time to kill" within ourselves whatever it is that hides us from ourselves and keeps at bay in us the one, great, saving endeavor of human life, the power to forgive in others what we do not find in ourselves.

Among the Hasidic tales one stands out for its compassion. "Once upon a time," the tale tells, "the Jews of a very pious congregation criticized their rabbi for giving money to the town ne'er-do-well whose use of the coins, the people knew, would not be for good. 'What?' the rabbi said, 'Shall I be more finicky in the giving of this coin than was God who gave it to me?'"

What we need to kill in life may not be sin at all. What we may really need to avoid like the plague may be the temptation to a bare and brutal sinlessness that threatens us with heartlessness, the greatest sin of all.

A TIME TO
BUILD UP

R evolutions are strange things. They give us a wild sense of triumph and, at the same time, they confront us with the fragility of victory. At the very moment a revolution succeeds, all the dreaming ends and all the theories turn to dust and all the talking ceases. Suddenly, the fireworks go black in the sky. The dawn becomes daylight. The real work of revolution begins at the very moment the old world collapses.

Then, whatever the promises that fired the upheaval, they cease to be poetry and begin to be the cold, hard facts of popular politics. The hopes fade into expectations. Heroes turn to humdrum, and all the drum majors of the world are left without a band. When the revolution has been won, the task in life is no longer critique. There is no need then to lead the madding crowd to wish for brave new worlds. On the contrary, the crowds depend on them. They demand them. No, the task in life after the dramatic work of a revolution is over is not to envision possibilities; it is to make good on promises. The task in life after the revolution ends is to build up what has been torn down. The task in life when the last note of the march fades is to begin again. "Our grand business," Thomas Carlyle wrote, "is not to see what lies dimly at a distance, but to do what lies clearly at hand." It is dailiness now that demands the work, not of dreamers, but of doers.

It is easier said than done. Ask Noah. Navigating an ark through a storm is hardly a challenge. People know a storm when they see one and flee it blindly whatever way they must, however frightening the manner of retreat. Chaos knows no fear, no reason. What people will not think of doing in ordinary time, they do without thinking in difficult times. After all, arks float. Cramped quarters are better than no quarters at all. Sacrifice abounds at a time of social upheaval. Any amount of effort, all manner of endurance, is possible. Nothing is too much to ask of people for whom the good life has become more rumor than fact. But that kind of character outlives itself quickly, exhausts itself posthaste when the gust turns and the pressure falls. Then there is a condition worse than suffering, and that is peace.

No storm lasts forever. Sooner or later, every wind passes. Then the time comes to start over, to do better than before, to produce an alternative product—a finer idea, a truer system, a preferable institution, a gentler nation—than the one that preceded this one. It is a time of new creation, a leap into eternal darkness, a moment of truth. It is not a time for the weak and will-less. It is also seldom a time of high drama. The stuff of dull dailiness takes over now. Now the real work of the new creation begins.

Noah knew the situation only too well. Life may not have been good for him in Nod but it was at least familiar. It was at least stable. It was his roots and his identity, his past and his future, his personal piece of the planet. It may not have been its greatest moment, its finest era, perhaps, but it was, after all, his.

Who does not know the dilemma; who hasn't been in the situation? "This may not be the best place in the world," we say, "but it is better than most." So we put up with a great deal of mindless immorality masking as the human condition. We tolerate the intolerable in our personal lives until we have no other choice, until blindness gives way to vision, until our sense of justice outdoes our sense of complacency, until we cannot take our nation, our family, our business, our church for granted one minute longer. Now our choices clarify with frightening simplicity: we must either accept what is or we must do it better. That is precisely what happened to Noah. Faced with a choice between irreconcilable alternatives, he had to choose one. "I do not believe in a fate that falls on human beings however they act; but I do believe in a fate that falls on them unless they act," G. K. Chesterton wrote. The situation is a serious one.

"A righteous man," the Scripture calls Noah. And a foolish one perhaps. He heard the Word of God within himself and determined to leave a decaying world behind him. A noble endeavor, indeed, but a very lonesome one for a person who had grown up in the situation and had managed, obviously, to resist the impulse to change for so long. The social climate had not eroded overnight, after all. Someone, Noah among them surely, had seen the circumstances that spawned the cultural disintegration and corruption and decline for years and had chosen to ignore them.

Suddenly, Noah not only finds himself in strange territory that is literally over his head, but he finds himself alone in it as well. He becomes Noah of the cocktail-party circuit whose conversation is no longer acceptable; Noah, the dissenter on the staff; Noah, the parishioner whose parish priest considers him mad; Noah, the strange man-about-town with an idea too radical to be believed. Poor Noah. If we have ever done a thing in our lives just a hair's breadth ahead of the crowd, we know him all too well. We know the uncertainty that goes with being a visionary-without-portfolio while the crowds clamor for dry land in the middle of floodwaters thick with the debris of the past.

There comes a time, in other words, when criticism of the past is simply not enough. There comes a new moment in life when we must dedicate ourselves to creating the future. And that is hard, hard work.

At that moment, we discover the difference between rabble-rousers and leaders, between critics and prophets, between the malcontents in an organization and the monumentally committed. Unfortunately, the discovery is often made far too late in the game. In looking for light, we find that we have followed a shooting star that is without substance and on its way to nowhere.

Tearing down the Berlin Wall was one thing; going about the process of rebuilding a totally demoralized and disenfranchised people is entirely another. Deinstitutionalizing the mentally ill was one thing; emptying the city parks of the emotionally sick and unwanted who congregate there because the closing of psychiatric hospitals leaves them nowhere else to go has turned out to be entirely another. Desegregating educational systems by bussing children out of their neighborhoods was one thing; equalizing educational programs so that inner-city schools have the same kind of facilities and programs as the schools in the suburbs has been entirely another. Writing papers on the lay vocation was one thing; incorporating women and laity into the structures of the church has turned out to be a disheartening other. Proclaiming the demise of sexism was one thing; reshaping the patriarchal marriage has turned out to be the formidable other. No doubt about it: revolution is the easy part. Rebuilding is the spiritual gift.

Rebuilding is one of the charisms of creation. This time, however, God does not do the recreating; Noah does. It is Noah's task now to save the human race from the disaster it has made of it. God does not wipe the world out and create it anew out of better material this time. On the contrary. God simply sends someone else to try again with the very same kind of creatures that were used in the first creation. And therein lies the lesson. To rebuild means to do it with the very same people who corrupted a situation in the first place, if not by debauching it themselves, at least by going along with the tide.

The obstacles to rebuilding, to renewing, to revitalizing a decadent system, then, are transparent ones. In the first place, we ourselves are products of the last system. Finding the openness of heart to imagine the possibility of a full gospel, a just world, an honest government, a nonsexist institution, a marriage of equals, a church where there is really "no Jew nor Greek, no slave nor free, no male nor female" muddles the mind. We are as crippled as what crippled us. Only we do not know it. And if we can bring ourselves to propose such a system, we can almost never imagine what the world would look like without the essential features of the old one. We stew in the juices of the past and want change, but what we really want is "planned" change; we want revolution as long as it's a "nice" revolution, or we demand a "new" world but not too new a world. We are by nature victims of the blindness of our own making, not rebuilders at all.

Rebuilding takes a peculiar kind of courage as well. It takes a gambler's heart and makes it holy. Rebuilders have to be willing to lose because they do not have a clue what it really means to win or where they're going if they do. They must be prepared to stumble around from failure to failure—from raven to dove—until something finally works and people are finally safe again, finally better off than they were before, finally free enough of the past to create life anew. To be a rebuilder means to risk failure time and time again, means to risk the support of the crowd you set out to save, means to be left in the dust as a crazy-eyed charlatan or a starry-eyed visionary, both useless, both dangerous. Guizot said of this dimension of the process of social change, "It is only after an unknown number of unrecorded labors, after a host of noble hearts have succumbed in discouragement, convinced that their cause is lost; it is only then that cause triumphs."

Rebuilding means to launch an entire people into space without a map and no way whatsoever to land again if and when anything goes wrong with the trip. So much for the French Revolution; so much for the great Communist experiment; so much for poet-princes in a politician's world. Once a person starts down the road of revolution, rebuilding becomes the price of perception and the cost of the dream. And woe to those who fail.

There is great spiritual merit in being a rebuilder, though. Rebuilders are those who take what other people only talk about and make it the next generation's reality. These are the superstars of the long haul. These are the people who pay with their lives to make an idea an actuality. They give up prestige and money and being the Peter Pans of the public arena for the long, hard struggle of turning their personal little worlds on their tiny axles. They build the new world right in the heart of the old. They begin to use altar girls when the first girls ask to serve. They start to provide social service and compassionate presence to AIDS patients at the first sight of suffering, whatever the moral conclusions of the moralists around them. They show us the world that the rest of us do not want to see until, forced to see it, we can ignore it no longer.

Some people go through life dispensing ideas that they never then bother to enflesh or that they abandon at the first hint of opposition. Armchair critics sprinkle their judgments liberally through life and then move on quickly to criticize the next effort of the next persons who, Noah-like, embark on a braver path. They always know what's wrong with any element of the human estate. They seldom, if ever, on the other hand, provide a better solution to the problem themselves. Their forte is questions, not answers. Rebuilders, on the other hand, show a better mettle.

To the rebuilder, life is one long spiritual exercise in cocreation. Sanctification depends for them on doing, always doing, whatever is necessary to prod the world one step closer to the reign of God, one idea nearer to the vision of God, one moment closer to the will of God.

Rebuilders are artists of the soul who shape a piece of human creation and leave the results to the kiln of time. They do not claim to have all the answers. They claim to honor the questions. They are prepared to float forever, if necessary, to find a better world, to shape a finer piece of the planet.

No amount of ridicule can discourage the rebuilders. No degree of rejection deters them. Rebuilders have a goal in life too finely honed to be abandoned for something so sniveling as thoughtless censure. But ridicule, rejection, and censure are commonly their kingdom nevertheless. For the zealots of the society, they are too slow. For the conservatives of the group, they are too fast. For the orthodox of the world, they are heretics. Their lot is too often, too plainly a lonely one. They are followed as heroes by some and tracked as traitors by others. They die as failed messiahs and vanquished enemies. They cannot possibly succeed because what they set out to build is not the damaged structures of a people seeking shelter but the plastic hearts of a people gone too long without anything of substance to love. They work with a people who know what was wrong with what went before but who are, at base, bereft of the longevity of spirit it will take to replace it with better.

Rebuilders face grey roads on dark nights that go nowhere that anyone has ever seen.

The soul of a rebuilder is based on the ability to look lovingly into nothingness and know that there is something there worth going to, worth giving this life to doing so that the lives of those that follow can be better still.

Rebuilders are commonly misunderstood, misjudged, and misnamed. They are called "reformers," "liberators," and "leaders," when, as a matter of fact, they are simply lovers gone wild with hope. Consequently, rebuilding is a sad but glorious task. Many the rebuilder who has died with a broken heart, sure that they had failed when the truth of the matter is that one lifetime is simply not enough span for anyone to succeed in reconstructing an entire culture gone to dust. Rebuilders are those characters of history who rise long after their deaths in the purple haze of tenacity. Eventually the world remembers them as the rethinkers, the redefiners, the rejuvenators of the world who carried it across the broken bridges of the past to the empty shores of a tenuous new era. Too late for the rebuilder then to know the beauty of being determined beyond all proof of possibility but not too late for the rest of us. In the rebuilders of the world, the rest of us can see the power of vision and the implacability of prophetic patience when our own lives seem to have stumbled and stalled. Rebuilders teach us that "courage is fear that has held on one minute longer."

Rebuilders look to the rainbow with the eye of a Noah. They intend to save as well as to flee, to begin as well as to end, to repeat the good things of life in a higher key. They do not deter easily, and because of them the human spirit has lived on from one human fiasco to the next, always better, always with the faith of the unfalteringly simple who have heard the Word of God and been foolish enough to believe, as George Bernard Shaw said, "This is the true joy in life, the being used for a purpose recognized by yourself as a mighty one; the being thoroughly worn out before you are thrown on the scrap heap; the being a force of Nature instead of a feverish selfish little clod of ailments and grievances complaining that the world will not devote itself to making you happy."

A Time to
Embrace

S cripture is full of the coming together of opposites—Joseph and his brothers, Moses' mother and Pharaoh's daughter, Jesus and the Samaritan woman, the young woman Mary and the old woman Elizabeth. In every case, something physical, something powerful happens: Joseph weeps at the sight of his jealous brothers, Pharaoh's daughter lifts the child from the river and entrusts him to the arms of his Hebrew nursemaid, Jesus drinks water from a forbidden bucket, Mary and Elizabeth burst into wild song at the thought of the power within them and its meaning for others. Scripture, in other words, is filled with one person recognizing, welcoming, embracing, and releasing the strength of the unfamiliar other. Everything that happens there, with very few exceptions, happens because people—modest, ordinary, confused, and very unlike people—find strength in one another to do what is beyond their simple selves. They meet and embrace. They meet and their souls touch. They meet and feel strongly. Then, because of that embrace and those feelings, the world changes on the spot.

But that's Scripture. We, on the other hand, are much more rational than that. We meet and make rules. We meet and make enemies. We meet and stay permanently separated. We put men on one side of the room; women on the other. We put whites on one side of the tracks; people of color on the other. We settle the money changers at the board room tables, the peons on the curbstones outside. We classify the footnote-gatherers at one level of humanity; the feelers at another.

What we really value in life, we are very clear to point out, is intelligence. We call it "rational." Men have it, whites have it, the wealthy have it, and academicians have it, we are taught. The rest of humanity simply limps along, feeling its way from indignity to indignity, unheard, unrespected, and essentially unvalued. In such a situation, what the body knows beyond theses and theories gets short shrift indeed. The fully human in us we debase and call it progress.

When the feelers wanted out of Vietnam, we called it treason. When the feelers find nuclearism obscene, we change the name of it to "Star Wars" and appropriate even more money to the planned destruction of the globe. When the feelers weep over whole armies gunned down running through a desert for home and children deprived of fresh water and dying of cholera in the arms of their Arab mothers, we call it "knee-jerk liberalism." When a woman runs for president, we ask if she is "strong enough" to press the nuclear button, but we have yet to ask whether a male candidate is strong enough not to press it at all. We call the intention to destroy the human race "resolve" and a desire to negotiate forever in order to protect it "soft." It is a pitiable dilemma. We are at an unhappy pass in the human condition when being human is the only thing that does not fit us for life.

We are a misguided people indeed. The question is why? The answer is that rationalism is irrational. We have thought our way into oblivion when what we really need is to feel our way into a new world order.

It is a mean, mean national spirit that can reason its way out of welfare for the poor and into welfare for the rich. The most civic of us resent welfare fraud but say not a word about paying more taxes to salvage the owners of the fraudulent Savings & Loan system. We pay more personal taxes to absorb the burdens not paid by tax-free corporations but refuse to raise the millage it will take to put decent schools in inner-city districts. We blush for shame at our feelings and live without shame at what our inhuman rationalizations have brought to the human condition. We crow about reason as the height of human definition and do to one another what no animals would do. Something has gone wrong in a society that accepts that kind of thinking and calls it "logical."

What's worse, at the level of the intellect we know there is something wrong with all of that, but at the level of feeling we feel very little at all. We watch inhumanity seep out of the edges of our kitchen television sets while we prepare canapes and hors d'oeuvres and never feel a thing. When it comes right down to it, thanks to our glorification of reason and the rational, we embrace very little except ourselves.

We need to rivet our attention, one element at a time, on the implications of Ecclesiastes for a world bent on instant satisfaction and total control, for a world where nothing is allowed to go wrong, though so much has for so many, for a world where the cornucopia is tipped and tilted to one end of the earth, and that end starving spiritually, while the other end, weak and wanting, is starving physically. And we watch it all without feeling a thing.

The obstacles to the development of feeling are many, and the effects of the loss of them on the development of life are multiple. It is very possible, in fact, that so intent have we become on "objectivity" that we have substituted thought for reality. We adopt the position that feelings can be out of control and avoid them like the plague. We fail to see that those who can possibly think that holocaust purifies and sexism protects and power empowers and systems save are the ones who are really wildly out of control. What purifies and protects, empowers and saves us lies hidden in the human heart where feelings rage and, in a tender irrational moment, people embrace without fear.

But it is precisely our love of systems, our respect for artificial order—for borders and rank and potentates and hierarchies—that knots our hearts beyond all respect for what is really the height of human achievement. We give over our minds and squelch our feelings in the face of those who say they know best for us and, in the process of being "rational," lose sight of the glory of human tenderness. With border struggles seething around him in pre-World War I Europe, the poet Thomas Hardy wrote,

> I shot him dead because—
> Because he was my foe,
> Just so: my foe of course he was;
> That's clear enough; although
>
> He thought he'd 'list, perhaps,
> Off-hand-like—just as I—
> Was out of work—had sold his traps—
> No other reason why.
>
> Yes; quaint and curious war is!
> You shoot a fellow down
> You'd treat, if met where any bar is,
> Or help to half-a-crown.

Unreasonably reasonable, we take up arms against people that we would never call enemy in any other situation and call it patriotic, moral, just, necessary. In caring more for our systems than our hearts, we delay the development of humanity to such a point that we may never really have time to become human at all before we manage to destroy our rational selves in one final and glorious burst of technological irrationality. It is to such insane assumptions about patriarchy and profit and personal achievement that we surrender our children in the schoolrooms of our world.

I remember all too well that day and moment when I first heard a teacher say that one of the advantages of war was "population control." I was horrified even then but too conditioned to say so. More than that, I am horrified now. Not at them but at me. The really horrible thing is that I wrote it down on the test, got it "right," starred in the course, and, years later, passed it on to another generation of students. And I never even had the grace to blush. Mighty reason had struck a blow against my humanity, and I never even had enough unpolluted humanity left in me to cry aloud at this scourge of reason, this sin against sweet reason, the scars of reason that I had absorbed, accepted, been afflicted with in the name of intellectual development and citizenship and authority.

The real problem, of course, is that it looks to us as if by such standards of rational barbarism we have triumphed. The real truth may be, however, that we have only managed by such worship at the monuments of reason to bring ourselves and our whole civilization with us to the brink of disaster, to our own premature demise. "Reasonable people," George Bernard Shaw says, "adapt themselves to the world; the unreasonable ones persist in trying to adapt the world to themselves. Therefore, all progress depends on the unreasonable." It is a lesson far too long unlearned.

We have made our nemesis ourselves. We have enshrined the

tenets of dualism and made the stirrings and promptings and feelings of the human body suspect. We have made anger a more acceptable emotion than love. We have warned people away from the urgings of their physical selves so that they could cultivate the obscenities of unfeeling reason. We have honed blind thought to such a fine point that to this day, in the richest country of the world, we can walk over the homeless and never see them, create the policies that leave people hungry and never question them, substitute rugged individualism for human community and call it holy.

Autonomy and independence, domination and control, separation and self have been carried to extremes, to the point that we have lost our capacity to love. We have failed to embrace because we have not been taught to embrace. And we have been dying, literally dying, from it as a people and a human population in our century. In Rwanda, in Bosnia, Iraq and Afghanistan, in the Pentagon and the board rooms and the slums of every city in the United States. Thousands upon thousands die and we have learned not to notice, not to protest, not to get "involved," not to feel. Psychic numbing has become our way of life.

What we need to develop in our time is a spirituality of embrace, the sanctification of feeling. We have been told that the greatest of these is love, but we do not really believe it. Not on the rational level. We have been told to be willing to repeatedly turn the other cheek but we do not risk it. Not on the social level. And yet, until we have the grace to regurgitate at the sight of brutality anywhere, what hope can we possibly have for the success of divinity's great experiment—the mind of God in the human heart.

Santayana writes: "The young man who has not wept is a savage and the old man who will not laugh is a fool." The spirituality of embrace depends on our willingness to put down the trappings of false intellectualism, of rationalism, of patriarchy so that both men and women alike can draw on their emotions without shame and be directed by their noblest feelings without fear.

Human community and globalism hang in the balance. The values we bring to decision making in the modern world are no longer a matter of purely private or personal importance. We cannot pretend to humanity and continue to deprive ourselves of half our way of perceiving at the highest levels of function. Governments without feeling are perverted at the center; people without feelings are monstrous mistakes.

To embrace the other, to take the stranger into our lives, to trust that the other is motivated by the same cares and loves as we are redesigns the human race. When we open our minds to the idea that the other feels our feelings, Japanese cease to be sinister; blacks cease to be dangerous; whites are no longer the incorrigible colonial dictators of the world. Shakespeare knew the spiritual discipline well. The Shakespearean character Shylock, a Jew in a virulently anti-Semitic Christian world, says, "I am a Jew. . . . Hath not a Jew hands, organs, dimensions, sense, affections, passions; fed with the same food, hurt with the same weapons, subject to the same disease, healed by the same means, . . . as a Christian is? If you prick us, do we not bleed?"

It is the ability to allow human feeling to become a reputable foundation for decision making at the highest levels that engenders the necessary antidote to a depraved rationalism. For too long have we allowed a false masculinity to guide the judgments of the church and justify the character of the corporate world and engorge a suicidal militarism and direct the policies of governments and reduce humanity to the rationalization of objectivity and deny the people of the world the validity of the feminine, of the feelings, in both women and men.

Reason has become the human sin; independence and individualism our pathology. Facts we have aplenty. It is feeling that we lack.

The time to embrace is now, before autonomy destroys community and leaves us less human at the end of our evolutionary process than when we began. Adoration of the rational has not worked. Only embrace can save us now.

The rabbis are quite direct about it. Rabbi Moshe Leib taught: "How to love is something I learned from a peasant. He was sitting in an inn along with other peasants, drinking. For a long time he was as silent as all the rest, but when he was moved by the wine, he asked one of the men seated beside him: 'Tell me, do you love me or don't you love me?' The other replied: 'I love you very much.' But the peasant replied: 'You say that you love me, but you do not know what I need. If you really loved me, you would know.' The other had not a word to say to this, and the peasant who had put the question fell silent again. But I understood. To know the needs of the other and to bear the burden of their sorrow—that is true love." And it was not learned in the *schul;* it was learned in a tavern, over wine, where feelings overflowed and facts did not count at all.

A Time to
Reap

The trouble with success is that very few people really know what it is. The *Tales of the Hasidim* make the point very clearly: Once upon a time the yehudi said to the disciples, "It's no great trick to be a worker of miracles; anyone who has reached a certain spiritual rung can shift heaven and earth—but to be a Jew, now that's difficult!" To gather the baubles of life, in other words, makes for only one kind of success; to live life well, to do what must be done, to be what we say we are day after tiresome day, makes for entirely another.

It is very tempting to romanticize reaping. We forget when we talk about reaping that reaping itself constitutes hard, hard work. Reaping takes place in hot sun, in short time periods, under great pressure, with no assurance whatsoever that what we gather will actually move in the market. We may reap a crop that no one wants. We may cut a field that brings no return. We may face a work that in the end will seem to fail. A great many crops are reaped that never sell. A great many fields are plowed under despite the quality of the crop.

The choice to reap is an enormous one. When the field we labored to seed shoots into bloom, we face a field of new work, not a cornucopia of trinkets waiting simply to be plucked and played with at leisure.

Reapers bend their backs simply to finish their work, not to assure themselves of success. The fields they plowed and planted, they complete; that is all. No more, no less. Reaping and personal success.

For those who consider achievement success, life is a lost art unless what we win is the thing we sought—the prestigious position, the financial security, the popular acclaim, the social status symbols, and the collection of cheap trophies. For those who consider the aims of life to be more important than the attainments of life, the questions more important than the answers, success depends more on what we value than on what we gain, more on the goal than on the prize, more on quality of life than on a concentration of things. For these, success has more to do with the fulfillment of our promises than on the guarantee of profit for ourselves.

Growing something, "working miracles," is no trick at all. The trick lies in going on with or without any palpable gain. The feat lies in going on doing what we know needs to be done simply because we must do it. The fulfillment of life lies in becoming more and more every day what we say we are. Success lies in being true to ourselves whatever the cost at the end of it all.

But that is not what we are taught in a profit-oriented society. The teaching that undergirds this society twists and squeezes the life out of life, drains it of meaning, and cements it in personal gain. "It is always sound business to take any obtainable net gain, at any cost and at any risk to the rest of the community," the economist

Thorstein Veblen wrote. The creed of stocks and bonds, profit and loss, interest rates and margins-of-return rings more clearly than the gospel and colors our spiritual thinking as well as our public policies. It affects us as persons, not simply as a population. We do what works, not necessarily what should be done. As a country we fight "sensible" wars with weapons that we know destroy more than defend. Yet we shrink from risking the dangers of nonviolent resistance that might also destroy us, yes, but that we know would at least leave the world intact at the same time. We keep spiritual "rules" that endanger the Word of God among us by preferring denominationalism in one period or Nazism in another period or sexism in our own age to the clear principles of Jesus. Obedience, we have come to know, requires a great deal less of us than conscience. We construct a merit theology built on rules for getting to heaven rather than a conscience built on the contemplative adherence to the will of God. We go for money and markets and cheap labor rather than for justice and the development of the whole human race. We sow legalism and chauvinism and institutionalism and wonder why it is that we have reaped a punishing parochialism, an oppressive patriarchy, a delimiting racism, and an obscenely stultifying sexism proclaimed in the name of God. We choose for systems and social profit rather than for holiness and globalism and the gospel of lepers and Lazarus. Worse, we call it success.

Because we have warped the notion of success in a society bent on tangible gains rather than spiritual goods, one of the characteristics of our time is the temptation to quit whatever does not yield an immediately clear profit. People spend their lives searching for fast-track positions or academic degrees designed to bring high salaries rather than deep human satisfaction. We train students for technology and business rather than for liberal arts and philosophy. We raise our children to be successful rather than cultured.

We want quick profit and immediate gratification, achievements and grain in barns. What we cannot count, we will not spend ourselves in getting. We want results and we want them now. We want guarantees, not possibilities. But such is not the charism of the reaper.

Reapers harvest for the sake of harvesting. They do what must be done, with little thought for profit, simply because it is work whose time is now. We are reapers when we do what the times demand, when we follow a process through to the end, whatever the final effects. Reapers marched for desegregation in Selma to assure the season of a moment whose time had come. Reapers sensed the deadliness of errant defense policies and, demanding the end of nuclearism, made the discussion of the subject a moral imperative for the first time in modern history. Reapers realize that patriarchy is doomed in society and press the idea of women's rights in a patriarchal church, not just for the sake of women but so that the idea of God can itself become a matter of theological debate. Reapers see the world in front of them and set out to harvest each painful moment in the passage of time so that moments to come can be better ones.

Reaping is a personal task as well as a public responsibility, however. In a world where life is a series of seasons, what we do least well, perhaps, is to reap the good times of our own lives. We talk about vacations that we never take. We plan family parties that we never give. We miss the weddings and skip the funerals and forego the school reunions and send cards instead of going to the graduations and the jubilees where old ties would be renewed and life could pass before our eyes in a panoply of gentle glory. So much dies in the fields of our lives that we never reap, both publicly and personally.

Reaping makes virtue of time. What we do not reap when the

time is full for it, rots in the center of our hearts. The problem is that once the moment is missed, we can never reclaim it again. Oh, we can celebrate every birthday late, of course. We can give Christmas day a nod and a wink, yes. We can tell everyone we meet on the street that we will someday soon be calling them and never do it. But promises and parting remarks of love and care do not substitute for presence and the slow, grinding process of becoming fully alive, one season of life at a time. And so, we miss the fruits of life; we lose its harvest of intervals accomplished; we live without thought of either the purpose or the meaning of the present period of life. We never ask why we are doing what we are doing and so, as a result, we never get to celebrate it when it achieves itself almost despite us. Like worker bees we concentrate only on what is in front of us. We plant with energy, yes, and we cultivate well, of course, but we too seldom seem to know when one phase of life has finished and so we fail to appreciate the start of the next one. Through it all, life passes us by. We do not even know it. Worse, far too often, we dread it.

People fear retirement because they do not know the beauty of reaping. People fear change because they do not value the process of reaping.

Two qualities in particular are obstacles to reaping. One is the temptation to temporize with discontent, the other is a lack of respect for each phase of the human enterprise.

The fact is that we are always waiting for the perfect time to do a thing. But it is never really the perfect time to do anything. So we wait. We wait for the right time to have the difficult conversation. We wait for the right time to make the changes that everyone knows are inevitable but that no one wants to see in their lifetime. We wait for the children to grow up before we sell the house that is too big to keep. We wait for the inheritance to enable us to leave the jobs that are wasting our souls and drying up our lives. We wait and we wait and we wait. In the meantime, while we linger along the way hoping for everyone to understand and approve of what they cannot understand until they know it, nothing changes. The harvesting of which we could have been a part is put off in hope of another day, a braver soul. Thoreau describes the process in stark terms: "We must walk consciously only part way toward our goal," he writes, "and then leap in the dark to our success."

For those who believe in reaping, success is not simply the harvest; it is the work itself. It is having a goal worth giving oneself to, whether it ever comes to pass or not. It is a willingness to go beyond what we are sure of to what is yet, at best, only a dark but golden dream. Success depends on the leap in the dark, on taking the chance that this moment is the right moment for us to do what we must do if we are ever to be worth being alive at all.

There is another obstacle to reaping, which is perhaps even stronger than the impulse to temporize. The major obstacle to reaping does not come from wanting the perfect future. The major obstacle to being able to enjoy the reaping times of life lies in our attachment to the past. We cling to time. We prefer what we were to what we are. We want the unfinishedness of interminable youth or the wild abandon of adolescence or the candy-store atmosphere of young adulthood. We want to freeze time in a series of unfinished moments. We refuse to let go of the dark hair and the firm waistline and the all-night parties of an earlier age for the silver-grey character of life after storms and the ample contentment of life after ambition or the early morning sunrises in the chair on an old porch. We don't reap because we won't grow. We simply stand in place, holding fast to the perpetual persona we have defined for ourselves and refusing to permit life to go on living in us. Ageism is simply our fear of our own mortality. Ageism is a reaper's menace.

Images of the aged in this society are clear ones, painful ones: age, this culture implies, sentences a person to shameful deterioration. Old people, they show us, are doddering and dull with nothing to say and nothing to do that is either worth doing or worth attending to. The faces of the mocking young and the tolerant middle aged who respond to them with condescending patience or irritated boredom demonstrate to the extreme that to be old is to be no longer relevant. Older people—people over fifty apparently—lack understanding, lack joy in life, lack purpose, lack value.

But reapers know that there is nothing farther from the truth than the notion that age diminishes life. On the contrary. Age is the reaping time.

In age, the ambitions that impel our middle years give way to a sense of inner achievement. Things outside ourselves lose their power to mask who we really are. What is inside of us—the learnings, the love—becomes what really enriches life. Enough becomes enough when the grasping years finally subside. Wisdom becomes a by-product both of success and of the failures that life has dealt in random ways. Love becomes something we give as well as something we receive, a mellow moment that takes the edge off wanting lesser things.

The road behind us becomes what freed us for the road ahead.

We know what counts now; we also know what doesn't. We harvest all the thoughts, all the ideas, all the beliefs we were trained in—and smile at them benignly. They do not control us now; we control them. We no longer need to know the unknowables. We learn, finally, just to be. The cult of the body gives way to the culture of the mind. The hysteria stops. The angers subside. Social life gets more real than political, and every day becomes fresh and free, a gratuitous gift not to be squandered, not to be missed.

Age is the period in which we harvest life, reap its good, and winnow its chaff without worry and without guilt. Now we know that everything we did was, in the end, of a piece. A series of twisted relationships has taught us to fear no one. A plethora of failures has taught us that nothing can really destroy us. A streak of great good luck has demonstrated as clearly as our errors how really little control we can claim over anything. It is age that teaches us how, freed from false guarantees about tomorrow, we can finally let go and live life well today.

We adore youth but disparage old age. We love the learning period of early adulthood but ignore the experience that comes with maturity.

The spirituality of reaping, then, lies in creating a new definition of success. Reaping is the talent for letting things grow to full stature and be finished. Success comes, as a result, not so much with knowing that we have controlled or conquered everything we have set out to do, but with finishing the stage before this one gracefully and with courage for the next.

The spirituality of reaping demands that we move through life from one point to another, never grasping, never clinging to the past. Buoyant youth jades easily in middle age; a middle-age attitude is small treasure in old age. What we need more than incompleteness cemented in time is the grace to live this present moment as if it were only a rich prelude to the next one. An open-handed hold on now makes reapers of us all.

Finally, the spirituality of reaping propels us from challenge to challenge in life with a laughing soul and a trusting eye. The reaper lives from season to season in perpetual hope. The reaper never ceases to plant again. "There is no failure except in no longer trying," Hubbard wrote. "There is no defeat except from within, no really insurmountable barrier save our own inherent weakness of purpose." The reaper's sense of purpose enlivens every generation, raising questions, resisting easy answers, refusing false success.

Reapers work from dawn to dark—without tiring, without guarantee of ever getting finished in time but with sure faith in the value of what they reap. They give a reaper's heart to everything they do and let those who come after them glean and grow because of those who reaped before them. "Never give up," the reaper says. "Never let a moment lie fallow. Never let a single sheaf of life go unground, unbound, unnoticed. Live every minute to the full."

Rabbi Moshe taught: "In this day and age, the greatest devotion, greater than learning and praying, consists in accepting the world exactly as it happens to be."

It is a reaper's world. Whatever you do, don't miss it.

A Time to
Weep

The mind revolts at the thought of it. A time to weep? A time? Never. This is the good-time generation, the land of jacuzzis and early retirement, the world of aspirin and analgesics, of alcohol and cocaine. This is the age of Disneyland and Six Flags over Anywhere and Everywhere. The signs are clear: suffering is not welcome here. But do not be fooled.

On this planet, psychic numbing has been raised to high art. This people avoids pain and misery, in others as well as in themselves, at all costs. This is not a people who braves grief in the face and stares it down. No, this people dedicates itself to the elimination of pain—its own—and the aversion of pain—everyone else's. But grief comes nevertheless.

Tears fall despite the fact that we resist them so strongly. Weeping and wailing are heard everywhere in the land of milk and honey—from the unemployed and the underemployed who want basics they can't have; from the divorced and abandoned who can't cope with what they do have; from the sick and the lonely who feel they have nothing to live for at all; from the beaten and the powerless whose lives are faceless and unrecognized; from the privileged and the well-to-do who have it all and still have nothing that really satisfies.

Unfortunately, few of us see our weepings as a spiritual gift or a matter of divine design. But we are wrong. Weeping is very holy and lifegiving. It sounds alarms for a society and wisens the soul of the individual. Ecclesiastes may be nowhere more correct than here. There is definitely a time for weeping. If we do not weep on the personal level, we shall never understand humanity around us. If we do not weep on the public level, we are less than human ourselves.

The Rabbi Honokh said it well: "The real exile of Israel in Egypt was that they had learned to endure it." There are, in other words, some things that ought not to be endured. There are some things worth weeping about lest we lose our sense of self. We must always cope with evil, of course, but we must never adjust to it. We must stay eternally restless for justice, for joy. Restless enough to cry out in pain when the world lacks them.

There are some things about which, if we do not weep, we will betray the human race. "If we had been better people," John Templeton said, "we would have been angrier oftener." Anger, disillusionment, tears explode in the midst of humanity to give us all a chance to become more human than we could ever have been without them.

If we do not allow ourselves to face and feel pain, we run the risk of entombing ourselves in a plastic bubble where our lies about life shrink our hearts and limit our vision. It is not healthy, for instance, to say that massive poverty is sad but "normal." It is not right to say that sexism is unfortunate but "necessary." It is not human to say that war is miserable but "essential." It is not healthy to insist that our deep hurts and cutting disappointments and appalling losses and great personal mistakes do not exist. On the contrary. To weep tears of frustration about them may be to take our first real steps toward honesty, toward mental health, toward a life that is worth living.

Weeping, in fact, may be the best indicator we have of what life is really all about for us. It may be only when we weep that we can come to know best either ourselves or our worlds. What we weep for measures what we are. What we weep over indicates what others may expect of us in life. It was when Jesus wept over Jerusalem that the die was cast, not for crucifixion, but for the blaze of energy and the boldness of stature that spent everything in him to change what, in the end, though it could not be changed, could not be ignored either. Tears, you see, are more than sadness.

Sadness afflicts the center of the soul. It closes us in on ourselves. It weighs us down and burdens our steps. When a person weeps, though, it is not a private matter. Tears demand our attention. Weeping fractures the social protocol to such a degree that we realize, no matter how remote we ourselves may be from the feelings that provoked another's tears, that nothing will ever be quite the same between us again until the disjuncture is repaired and the rupture is healed. Tears warn us that the foundations of a relationship that we may have dealt with so cavalierly in the past are now in danger. Tears beg for a human response and dare not be denied.

Weeping signals that it is time to change things in life because for someone, somehow, life has now become unmanageable. "Though all afflictions are evils in themselves, yet they are good for us, because they discover to us our disease and tend to our cure," John Tillotson wrote. Without our tears, we have no hope of healing because we do not begin to confront the anguish.

Of all the expressions of human emotion in the lexicon of life, weeping may be the most functional, the most deeply versatile. The tears we weep show us our deepest, neediest, most private selves. Our tears expose us. They lay us bare both to others and to ourselves. What we cry about is what we care about. What we have no tears for hardens our hearts.

Without tears, self-knowledge is at best a fiction. We learn too late in life sometimes that laughter and tears come from the same place. We do not weep for everything we lose in life. No, we weep only for the loss of those things that have brought us our greatest joy. Clearly, where sorrow resides lies the clue to what we really love in life. When we cry after a quarrel, for instance, the source of those tears reveals the real nature of the argument, the real hope for reconciliation. To cry because we have hurt another reveals one thing; to cry because we feel the pinch of our own humiliation and psychological battering in the struggle unmasks entirely another agenda. Learning to tell the difference between the two makes the difference between a life lived in truth and a life lived in shadow.

When people deny their pain, it is almost always because they have not cried enough. "Being strong" and "keeping our chin up" may simply be excuses to avoid the unavoidable, to lie our way through life until we die, empty shells of ourselves and pale intimations of what it is to be fully human. What we do not choose to face, we cover with a thin coating of cold courage. But our tears betray us to ourselves and give us back the opportunity to be honest, at least within the recesses of our own aching hearts.

Weeping signals change as well as loss, though. The temptation is to confuse the two, to make them synonyms, to assume that one is always the other. Learning to let go in life takes great faith, great fortitude, true, but recognizing that we are at a transition point takes even greater abandonment. When the present ceases to fit and the future has yet no definition, tears oil the way between the two. Tears lead us from loss to change. Otherwise, we may cling to a past dead beyond recall. Tears give life to the grief of endings, give them dignity and give them honor. What was, was good. What is to come is mystery. Once the tears have been shed that mark the loss, then the changes can be made that mark the new beginning. Tears give presence and power to both in life. Without tears, change may never come because the loss may never be acknowledged.

Tears release us from the past. Weeping, Ecclesiastes knew, brings with it the therapy of disengagement. What gushes out of us in a torrent of tears has no more power to control us. What has been dulled by years of suppression, perhaps, comes tamed from its lair as a melancholy tear that, stripped of its secret chain, weighs down our hearts no more. The ungrieved deaths of our lives can finally go to rest once the tears come. The losses of life lose their sting in the clear stream of sorrow. The memory of hurts and rejections grown larger through the years shrinks to size in the water of tears. Tears cleanse and rinse and irrigate our souls so that new life can flow where only silt had been. They give us the right to grow beyond where we have been to a place where life beckons us to begin again.

Until we cry about what punctures our psyches—stand it toe to toe, wrestle it to the ground of our memories, staunch the blood of it—we will never get beyond the wounds. The process of human development demands, merits even, a tear or two. How else can we move from place to place, phase to phase of life, and mark the passages as we go? Perhaps the tears we weep at each crossroad in time are the only measure of value by which those moments can ever be judged.

But if, indeed, there is a time for weeping, then two questions rise to plague us and demand an answer if we are ever to make sense out of our lives. The first question calls us to weigh every act of life. It begs to know if any past we can leave without tears, with cavalier goodbyes and hardly a sigh—let alone a tear—was really worth doing at all. The second question is worse than the first. It wants to know when we look dry-eyed at the past if we learned anything in the doing of it that made life sweet enough to want to keep? They are questions to break the heart.

The ancients talked about the "gift of tears," the grace of sorrow for sin. Sin is not a popular concept these days, and sorrow is even more suspect in this culture. "We don't sin; we make mistakes," the respondents to a study of contemporary Christian beliefs report. We do not, the modern version holds, need to weep either for our own brokenness or for the damage we have done to others because, unfortunate as it may be, it was beyond our conscious control. As a result of thinking like that, we simply limp along from "mistake" to "mistake," taking responsibility for little and having concern for less. In the end, then, we may fail to identify the patterns of our lives that have us retracing ourselves in a series of steadily decreasing circles until we stand trapped in our own unreflective and unrewarding behaviors. We ignore the call to holiness in ourselves that consistent and constant struggle invites us to require. Worse, we ignore the effects of our lack of ethical principles on others.

To have the "gift of tears" is to have the heart to care about what we do to others, to have the conscience to care about what we have done to destroy creation, to have the commitment to self to care about what we have done to our bodies and our minds in the name of "freedom."

Tears attune us to ourselves and tears attune us to the rest of the human race as well. Once we ourselves have suffered, the suffering of others falls upon our softened hearts, and we become more human members of the human race. We learn that there are tears of joy as well as tears of sadness, and we allow ourselves to weep them. We learn not to fear weeping in the cause of strength because we come to know that unfeeling strength is bogus and conquered pain is strengthening. We come to realize that it is tears alone that stop us where we stand in life and demand that we assess it one more time, this time with the sort of reflection that sees more than anyone can see.

As necessary as tears may be, however, there are obstacles to weeping that drain life to the dry.

There is such a thing as a desiccated heart, a deadness of soul so severe that no amount of tears can penetrate its dried-out hide. When we hide our weaknesses under the cover of arrogance, that is desiccation too thick for tears. When we affect detachment and call emotional distance holy, that is desiccation too impenetrable for tears. When we sneer at feelings and make a god of the rational, that is desiccation too dense for tears. Then we turn to dust inside. We lose touch with ourselves and we ignore the needs of others. The desiccated heart betrays the human spirit with the spurious notion that what is strong is without feeling. "How was your strafing run tonight?" the reporter asked the young flyer in the Persian Gulf War. "Fantastic," the young man glowed on national TV. "It was a turkey-shoot! We blasted them as they ran!" It was nothing, in other words, to gun down an entire army running for their mothers' homes. It was tough, it was macho, it was patriotic to slaughter the defenseless. It was done with never a tear. It was done with a desiccated heart. "Jerusalem, Jerusalem," the Scriptures report of Jesus, "I have wept over you like a mother over her child." No room for the false-face of a fraudulent courage here. Jesus wept.

It is possible to be too superficial to cry. Young people, people whose emotions have yet to be formed by tears of their own, find it easy to laugh at tragedy, at affliction, at despair. Some older people, too, more skilled at looking mature, perhaps, but protected from the normal stresses and strains of life, can skate through their days and never deal with a real human emotion, the kind that leaves people different after they have suffered. They cry tears of petulance, but they have not cried tears of pain. They never suffer much in life, but they never grow much either.

Sterility and superficiality disease the soul and leave it too shriveled up to understand life, let alone enjoy it. Those who cannot weep cannot really laugh either.

Finally, there is the disease of self-pity, the process of wallowing and whining through life to such an extent that all our tears are cheapened. Once self-pity settles into the human soul, all of life becomes an exercise in unmitigated despair. Nothing is tragic enough to weep for; everything is too horrible to appreciate. The beauty of life is reduced to the casual. Perfection is taken for granted but never achieved. Criticism becomes the charism of the small-minded and inexperienced. The whole scenario clogs the soul. There is no weeping here; only complaining.

There is a spirituality of weeping, however, that stretches life to its outside edges and gives us a capacity for all its crannies, all its treasures. Those who live in holy anger know what it is to look at a wounded world and cry. Those who have cultivated humility and self-criticism know the pain of failing themselves and so can rise to even greater heights because their tears have made them whole. Those who live committed to honesty face the pain in life and do not flinch from it.

For those who develop the spirituality of weeping, however, life becomes a place of honest assessment and humble achievements, of keen love and desperate losses. Life matters to those who weep. Life goes on from moment to moment with an eye to loss, a heart for change, and a soul that craves justice and joy with the passion of desert land for water.

The rabbis tell that a man who was afflicted with a terrible disease complained to Rabbi Israel that his suffering interfered with his learning and praying. The rabbi put his hand on his shoulder and said, "Tell me, friend. How do you know what is more pleasing to God: your studying or your suffering?"

The answer, of course, is that it all depends on whether or not we know, really know, what weeping is about.

A TIME TO
REFRAIN FROM EMBRACING

I was too young to have language for it then, but I was very certain about the concept: the picture story of the Garden of Paradise that lined our first-grade classroom was some kind of cruel joke. Here was a God who put people into a haven of delights and then forbade them to taste the best of the fruits that surrounded them. "If you don't want them to have it," I thought, "why would you put it there in the first place?" Unless you wanted to tantalize people, of course. Unless you hoped to entrap someone, perhaps. Was this, I wondered, really a God who could be trusted?

The theological reflections of children can be irritatingly uncomfortable because they are irritatingly close to all the unspoken problems of religious education, all the real questions of the spiritual life. Children think with such clarity because they do not yet know enough of the packaged answers to make thinking impossible. Then, after years of intellectual conditioning, it takes ages before a person becomes really free enough once more, if they ever do, to risk those early ideas and concerns again. Unfortunately, those intervening years of trial and error, questions and rote answers wind through "a knowledge of good and evil" we might well have done better without.

If we had only looked a little more deeply, a little more sympathetically at the Scripture story of the Garden of Eden or at the scene on Mount Sinai—Israel's two great defining moments—we might have understood before it was too late that the prohibitions on what we see as goods were meant more for our development than for our personal destruction, more to make us happy than to hamper us in our thirst for life. God, the Garden Story is trying to say, is not tantalizing us; God is not trying to entrap us. God is trying to save us from ourselves. God, we learn with Moses on Sinai, is warning us in the giving of the ten commandments to beware of the worm in the apple, the undercurrent in every flowing stream, the burn of the sun, the blast of the wind, the urges in ourselves that leave us sated and unsatisfied at the same time. When Ecclesiastes cautions us that there is a time to refrain from embracing, it is asking us to learn that enough is enough.

It is begging us to understand that what is forbidden us sets us free. What really enslaves us, the text implies, is our propensity to make gods of what are not, to worship only our own wants and wills and wiles, to bury ourselves in stockpiling the toys of life, to exhaust ourselves in our lusts, to destroy everything around us, to satisfy everything within us that has been long out of proportion in the first place. We were warned in Eden and directed on Sinai, but we go on demanding our "knowledge of good and evil" and getting it—the hard way.

Scripture keeps trying to tell us that there are some sorts of knowledge that we would do well to do without. Scripture keeps trying to tell us that there will be things that look good to us that, if we peel away the beguiling externals and expose the underside of each of them, we would see that they carry within themselves seeds of inherent dissatisfaction. Not everything that looks good to us is good for us.

The greatest tragedies of life do not lie in being denied what we want. We can all survive what we have already learned to do without. No, the greatest difficulties of life often come instead from getting what we desire. It's when we get what we want that we have to determine what good it brings us, what good it withholds. It's then that we learn that what we "refrain from embracing" may be as important to the enjoyment of what we love as what we embrace with open arms.

In every good thing in life there is to be had a knowledge of both good and evil. Chocolate is good; too much of it is sickening. Trust is good; dependence is not. Ambition is good; compulsion is not. The problem arises when we choose to see only the good in good. The model who develops an eating disorder because it is good for a model to be thin has failed to reckon with the dark side of beauty. The social worker who loses touch with her own family because she is consumed by her work with the family of others has missed the meaning of her work as well. Beauty is good, but obsession with body size is an evil of immense dimensions. Concern for others is good, but disregard for our own emotional environment is an evil too pathetic to define. In both instances, too much of a good thing turns into evil. In both instances, good masks evil. In both situations, it looks at first as if we want one thing, when, as a matter of fact, if we examined our own hearts closely, it would be clear even to us that we really want another much lesser good. The model wants perpetual youth. The social worker wants a sense of personal achievement, perhaps, more than she wants healthy families, or she would be concentrating on her own.

The point is that we can make gods out of goodness, too.

When we distort a good, wrench it, inflate it, become consumed by it and no other, we ourselves turn good into evil. That's why there is, certainly, "a time to refrain from embracing." What we exaggerate in life, what we lose balance about, will eventually be our undoing. Like the mountain climber who dies in a snowstorm on a summit, we run the risk of destroying in ourselves the very things we love in life because we ignore in ourselves the signs of their perversion in us.

"Our own heart always exceeds us," the poet Rilke wrote. We outrun ourselves. We take on more than we can handle. We scoop to our breasts all the goods at our fingertips like children at a candy counter and wonder why we can't really enjoy, can't taste, can't savor any of them. We become engorged with good. And then it hurts.

The cult of the saints, even the very notion of sanctity if it means some kind of self-denial, has fallen into disuse in this culture. We do not emulate easily those who give up things of life. We are too busy amassing to respect the value of letting go. We do not admire greatly anyone we consider to be a denier of the "good things of life." In a society bent on consumption, simplicity of life is not a virtue, and that kind of asceticism is welcomed only with suspicion. If anything, it could all be a little sick, we think, a touch neurotic. After all, if a thing is there in front of us why not have it all?

But in that case, there is another kind of person who might bear watching in a society of affluence. In this day and age, the model of life that may have a more saintly effect on us in the long run may well lie in those who have it all and then wander aimlessly from place to place looking for more. More, more, more. Until dissipated, crazed, bored, restless, they come to realize that too much of a good thing is as denigrating of the human soul as deprivation itself.

They come to understand that what they lacked in life—the

ability to refrain from embracing—is what they needed most in life. And we need to learn that too. A sense of the presence of God consumes Moses on Sinai. When we fill the present with anything other than a sense of God, we will never, ever have enough. We will simply consume ourselves consuming.

The great spiritual task, then, is to look very diligently at that passion in us that at this very moment has become, under the guise of good, our greatest struggle. I must come to ask myself what it is that I have embraced that requires restraint if I am going to live a life that is whole and balanced. What good is it that is making all the other goods of life impossible for me to attain?

The problem is that we have been sent on a wrong route: the goal in life is not to become perfect. There is no such thing. The goal in life is to become good. That is an entirely different enterprise. The need to be perfect is what drives us to be first, to be best, to be in control, to own the field for ourselves. Perfection has started a lot of wars, executed a lot of people, led to a lot of suicides. Goodness, on the other hand, knows its limitations at the outset. Defended by a sense of fallibility, goodness lives lightly in the universe, walks softly through the world, brings patience to the task of growing, does not call one thing another, loves deeply and fails often, yes, but knows, in the end, what to refrain from embracing. Goodness does not give itself away to those undercurrents of the heart that enslave and take us captive from ourselves. Goodness is happy to do well. Goodness does not have to do it all.

"The basic test of freedom," Eric Hoffer wrote, "is perhaps less in what we are free to do than in what we are free not to do." The test is to know what we are really pursuing. We may, in fact, be pursuing security and call it community. We may really want achievement and call it education. We may really want control and call it love. Knowing what we are free not to do as we pursue the purpose of our lives must become the criterion by which we judge what we are doing at all times. We must be free not to do any good thing that would warp all the other good things in our lives. Free not to overwork; free not to overeat; free not to overdo; free not to overcontrol. The freedom to "refrain from embracing" may, in the final analysis, be the real secret to the good life.

The hard thing is that we too often realize our imbalances in retrospect. We always recognize the excesses of our past. We remember the period in which we were too lovesick to study. We know well when it was that we valued the car and the boat and the credit cards and the clothes more than we valued the job or the family or the relationships they represented. We have a hard time knowing—admitting—what we're wasting time on now, however. "No one is free who is not master of the self," Epictetus taught. But we go on. Passionately pursuing one type of good, we fail to ask what real good those things are denying us.

Important as it is to mental health and human happiness, the development of freedom of heart is not without obstacles.

The first obstacles derive from the fact that when we ask ourselves what is lacking in our lives, we do not know how to listen to our own internal answers. The second is that we find self-criticism painful. The third is that we assume that the assumptions of the world around us are correct.

If I work eighty hours a week and complete project after project and still feel unhappy, then achievement is not what I lack. What I lack and will not listen to in myself is the understanding that achievement is no substitute for rest or reflection or family or creativity. What I lack is the awareness that I will always lack something until I provide for those other things in my life.

If I do not examine my present life closely, if I do not make myself chart how I am using my time, I will never come to face what I need to resist in life. I will just keep on overdoing something, refraining from none of it, and turning one of life's great moments into straw. I must insist with myself on looking at the goals under my goals. I must insist on uncovering what I am getting out of my own destruction. I must demand of myself to know why I stay at what is not good for me, why I continue to do what I do not want to do, why I wear myself out straining for one thing at the expense of another that is equally good, equally important to the human condition.

If I do not question the assumptions upon which my life is based, I can never unmask what the bogus is all about. It is an assumption that women should stay in the home, so I stay in the home until there is no me left. I must ask who said so and to whose advantage are the rules that I live under in my heart. It is an assumption that militarism is a defense, so I keep on supporting military expenditures until the roads go to pulp and the schools go to seed and the medical standards of the nation are sold only to the highest bidders. It is an assumption that money makes for happiness and that the more money we have the more happiness we have, so I work and work and overwork and feel poorer by the day. It is all wrong. Terribly wrong.

"Even when I sit, the sun keeps shining, the grass continues to grow," the Zen Master teaches. There are things in life that go on without us despite whatever we do. There are some things that will happen whether we do anything or not. There are some things we can do nothing about. We are not the messiah. We can only do as much as we can do. Then we must be about the rest of what life is about. Then we must refrain from taking one thing to the point that there is nothing left for everything else in life.

The spirituality of refraining is the spirituality of balance. Balance smooths life out and makes life livable. It makes us human and makes us happy. We didn't need to eat from the Tree of the Knowledge of Good and Evil, you see. But we did. And we do. And we have suffered for it over and over again ever since. Socrates taught, "The fewer our wants, the nearer we resemble the gods." Eden and Sinai tell us quite powerfully that Socrates was right.

A TIME TO GAIN

Once upon a time some disciples asked their rabbi, "In the book of Elijah we read: 'Everyone in Israel is duty bound to say, "When will my work approach the works of my ancestors, Abraham, Isaac, and Jacob?"' But how are we to understand this? How could we in our time ever venture to think that we could do what they could?"

The rabbi explained: "Just as our ancestors invented new ways of serving, each a new service according to their own character— one the service of love, the other that of stern justice, the third that of beauty—so each one of us in our own way must devise something new in the light of the teachings and of service and do what has not yet been done."

It's a lovely story. The perspective it gives takes the burden of success off our shoulders and faces us instead with the task of creative responsibility. We are not asked to do more than we can. We are not asked to be someone else. We are simply asked to be ourselves and to do something in our own time that has value. We are asked to profit the world by our existence. We are allowed to be unique; we are not allowed to be useless.

The story of cocreation is the autobiography of every human life, both yours and mine. Responsibility for the world starts here, with you, with me. Life is not about traveling through. Life is about doing something that lasts beyond us, something that will, eventually at least, bring the world one step closer to completion. Life requires that we do more than philosophize about what the world lacks. We must do something of ourselves to provide it. Otherwise, why were we born?

This focus on A Time to Gain in Ecclesiastes, recalls a Scripture passage that is equally clear about this notion. The Twelve have labored on their boat all day long—heaving heavy, heavy nets out into the waves in the heat of the day and pulling them in empty, time after time after time. They have caught nothing where they would normally expect to find fish. But when, under the impulse of the Spirit, determined not to quit, in one last great effort, they cast out of the other side of the boat, they haul in a net full to overflowing. They gain because they refuse to quit trying. They gain because they try different ways of doing what must be done. They gain because they keep working together. And, in the end, they bring up more fish than they could possibly use for themselves. Because of their continued and creative efforts, life is better now, more secure now, for everyone. "Work," the Persian poet Gibran writes, "is love made visible."

The accent is on common effort and universal gain, not on simple "self-fulfillment" and not on personal profit. The meaning is clear: We do not work for ourselves and we do not work for nothing. We work so that others may not want. We work for the gain of the next generation. We are involved in the exercise of world-building, of cocreation and we must in each age work in new ways and in earnest and together.

Ecclesiastes puts it squarely. "There is a time to gain," it says. There is a time to make a difference. There is a time to develop the best in ourselves so that we can make the best possible world for everyone else as well.

The truth is that the most telling indicator of the spiritual deterioration of the Western world may be in its modern disregard for work. People work for money now, not for the sake of the work itself. People work so that they can do something other than work as soon as possible. People work because of economic necessity, not for the sake of creative expression. People work at compartmentalized tasks that have no meaning to them. And so, ironically enough, we have separated work and life. Work is something we do because we have to do it, not something that we want to do because it is in itself fulfilling, meaningful, life giving. We work hard, yes, but we don't begin to live until after the workday is over. We work now only because we must, not because we want to or because the work itself compels. We work for personal profit now; we do not work for human gain or human expression. It is a sad commentary on creation.

With motives like those directing us, though, it is possible to do anything of any caliber and never even realize the moral schizophrenia to which we have fallen ill. We have arrived at a world where people can work in nuclear arms plants and never feel an ounce of compunction about the potential effects of their work. We can work in places that dump chemicals in streams and rivers and lakes and seas without a quiver of conscience. We can spend our lives hyping cigarettes and hawking alcohol and dallying in false advertising and slick brochures about barren land and cheap trinkets and never for a moment wince at the waste. We can take "sick" days for vacation time with impunity and do sloppy work without chagrin and turn mornings into one long coffee break and accept a wage for doing it without so much as a thought. We have managed in our time to completely divorce our work from our lives. Then we wander listless for years, wondering what our lives were really all about. "We build statues out of snow," the poet Walter Scott says, "and weep to see them melt."

Yet some of the basic questions of life are "What am I doing and why am I doing it? Who profits from what I do and who does not? What difference does this work make to the coming of the reign of God?" The questions alone could change the world. They make us look again at the question of vocation and meaning, justice and complicity. They make us come face to face with new decisions about life and our own role in it. They force us to confront the myth of our own powerlessness. They bring us to the mirror of the world and ask us what we ourselves have done to make that world better or worse.

Work connects us to the rest of the world. It is our ticket to humanity, our permit to be alive. It is in our work that we share in a special way in the life of God.

Lurking within us, however, in the most hidden recesses of our souls, the obstacles to a spirituality of cocreation run deep. Comfort, alienation, powerlessness, and self-centeredness have a steel grip on the Western soul.

Capitalism, the notion that individuals can have what individuals can get, turns greed into virtue in this society. We resent subsidized housing, but we say hardly a word about the overruns and tax exemptions and sweetheart deals that keep corporate USA running. We criticize how the poor spend their food stamps but find no problem at all in the practice of cutting corners ourselves on every tax return form we submit. We forget that God will judge the poor on honesty and us on our generosity. Without realizing it, perhaps, we use the poor of other countries to provide the slave labor costs that will put cheap goods in our own stores and no goods whatsoever in theirs.

We would like a better world, but we ourselves go on sustaining this one by our silence, by our acceptance, by our assumption that what is now must ever be. Somehow the idea escapes this generation that we have the responsibility to change it, one heart at a time. What other ages took upon themselves as the work of their lives—to build a country or educate a people or change a government or convert a world—has somehow or other been lost to our own. The goals of this age, on the contrary, have become disturbingly small. Past ages worked for the good of their children. We work for ourselves and leave our children to correct what we will leave behind—garbage in space, garbage in our waterways, nuclear garbage in our landfills. In the making of our assembly-line money, we have lost the vision that makes for holy responsibility. Indeed, we need to develop a new concept of work in the world, and we need to do it with all the workers of the world. We need to recognize the morality of work and bring conscience to bear on our own.

Industrialization began the process that computerization now hastens at breakneck speed. Torn from the land, devoid now of creative manual labor, we no longer see the results of our work. We have gone from being farmers or craftspeople who nursed their products from furrow to market every step of the way with their own hands to being robots in a line of equally isolated robots. We do not make products anymore. We count rivets or we stack paper or we handle the coins or we sweep a part of the storeroom floor or we input segments of data. Compartmentalization has taken us over, limited our sight, robbed us of a view of what we are really doing in life. Serfs never had it so bad. Serfs saw a crop through from beginning to end, lived off of it themselves, canned it and planted it again. They knew the effects of what they did or didn't do, and they knew them in their own lives.

We, on the other hand, never see the fruits of our labor. We never really get to know the creative potential we have. We lose sight of the toxic wastes we create and the weapons we make and the corporate effects of slick deals and canny negotiations.

We don't work with people anymore. We simply work in their presence. We are on our own, doing minuscule tasks for giant corporations. We are pawns in a system of giants. It is hard to take responsibility for what we never see.

We despair of our powerlessness and go along because, we say, there is nothing else to do. We have lost our sense of importance to the human race.

But for those who can overcome the vortex of capitalist greed, the feeling of alienation from the system and the products they are producing, the sense of impotent anonymity, there is a spirituality of work waiting to be developed that can re-create this barren, starving world. "Ideals are like stars," Charles Schurz writes. "We never reach them, but like the mariners of the sea, we chart our course by them." It is the ideals of work that we are lacking. It is these ideals by which we must chart our lives and our work if either we or the world around us can ever hope to gain from our presence on earth.

A spirituality of work is based on a heightened sense of sacramentality, of the idea that everything that is, is holy and that our hands consecrate it to the service of God. When we grow radishes in a small container in a city apartment, we participate in creation. We sustain the globe. When we sweep the street in front of a house in the dirtiest city in the country, we bring new order to the universe. We tidy the Garden of Eden. We make God's world new again. When we repair what has been broken or paint what is old or give away what we have earned that is above and beyond our own sustenance, we stoop down and scoop up the earth and breathe into it new life again, as God did one morning in time only to watch it unfold and unfold and unfold through the ages. When we wrap garbage and recycle cans, when we clean a room and put coasters under glasses, when we care for everything we touch and touch it reverently, we become the creators of a new universe. Then we sanctify our work and our work sanctifies us. A spirituality of work puts us in touch with our own creativity. Making a salad for supper becomes a work of art. Planting another evergreen tree becomes our contribution to the health of the world. Organizing a good meeting with important questions for the sake of preserving the best in human values enhances the humanity of humanity. Work enables us to put our personal stamp of approval, our own watermark, the autograph of our souls on the development of the world. In fact, to do less is to do nothing at all.

A spirituality of work draws us out of ourselves and, at the same time, makes us more of what we are meant to be. My work develops myself. I become what I practice all my life. "Excellence," Samuel Johnson wrote, "can only be attained by the labor of a lifetime; it is not to be purchased at a lesser price."

By casting our nets one more time, by trying again when trying seems futile, we come to test the limits of our strength and know the mettle of our lives. Good work—work done with good intentions and good effects, work that upbuilds the human race rather than reduces it to the monstrous or risks its destruction—develops qualities of compassion and character in me.

My work also develops everything around it. There is nothing I do that does not affect the world in which I live. In developing a spirituality of work, I learn to trust beyond reason that good work will gain good things for the world, even when I don't expect them and I can't see them. In that way, I gain myself. Literally. I come into possession of a me that is worthwhile, whose life has not been in vain, who has been a valuable member of the human race. Finally, a spirituality of work immerses me in the search for human community. I begin to see that everything I do, everything, has some effect on someone somewhere. I begin to see my life tied up in theirs. I begin to see that the starving starve because someone is not working hard enough to feed them. And so I do. It becomes obvious, then, that the poor are poor because someone is not intent on the just distribution of the goods of the earth. And so I am. I begin to realize that work is the lifelong process of personal sanctification that is satisfied only by saving the globe for others and saving others for the globe. I finally come to know that my work is God's work, unfinished by God because God meant it to be finished by me.

When Rabbi Yaakov Yitzhak was young, his next-door neighbor was a smith who got up before dawn every morning and struck hammer to anvil with the roar of thunder. "If this man can tear himself away from sleep so early for worldly work, should not I be doing the same for the service of the eternal God?" the young rabbi asked himself. So the following morning he rose before the smith who, as he entered his smithy, heard the young man reading his prayers in a low, clear tone.

"Listen to him work," the smith said to himself. "I must be even more diligent because I work to keep my family, not simply to develop my mind." And on the following night the smith rose even earlier than the Hasidim.

But the young rabbi took up the challenge and won the race for concentration on his work. In later years he used to say, "Whatever I have attained I owe first and foremost to a smith."

Who, if anyone, owes their sense of sanctifying work to me?

A Time for
Peace

Nikos Kazantzakis wrote, "I fear nothing. I hope for nothing. I am free." It is a state devoutly to be wished, perhaps, but that is not the way we are trained to think. We have learned to fear everything. We are raised to hope for everything. We are too much enslaved to ourselves to be at peace.

I heard two children talking recently and began to understand with painful clarity what is implied by our desire for "the peaceable kingdom." I realized in their simple speech that we could not have peace until we each cultivated within ourselves a child with open arms. We could not have peace until we all sat down at the table of life intent on nourishing one another together. I also realized in the comments of the children that we are, in fact, doing just the opposite.

In one childish conversation about nationalities and historic feelings, I heard a microcosm of my world. And, as a result of it, I began to see clearly that even if we dismantled all the war machines of the world tomorrow, it would be no guarantee that we would have peace. The armies of the world, it dawned on me, simply demonstrate the war that is going on in our souls, the restlessness of the enemy within us, the agitation of the human condition gone awry. I was talking to the children, to the innocents, and they were not innocent of the wars that rage within us at all. They were, in fact, a kind of religious inkblot test of the society they breathe. They knew just whom to hate, and they knew it without nuance. They were Irish children, and they resented Americans for their money and hated the English for their history. "I hate them," the one child said simply. "Me, too," the other agreed. It was uncomplicated and it was clear. There was no talking them out of it. Schooled in facts, they were impervious to the poetry of the spirit. What was, was.

I saw in their faces all the children of the world. Hutu children and Serbian children and Palestinian children—children who were learning to hate Tutsi children and Bosnian children and Jewish children. They had all been born into a world of adult enemies, which they inherited along with the land under their feet. If truth were told, though, what they really inherit is not our wars but our enemy making, not our armies but our lack of honesty, not our problems but our lack of humanity. They had inherited the sins of their ancestors, and they lie like timebombs within their hearts, festering in the spirit of the world.

"Now people oppress people," a Chinese proverb teaches, "but after the revolution, it will be just the opposite." Obviously others before us have known the truth of peace. What makes for conflict is not necessarily a lack of resources resolved through the machinations of global struggle. No, what makes for conflict is the lack of peace within ourselves. To the restless, the empty, the parochial, the patriarchal, petty little wars are the music of their conflicted souls, and what they do not inherit they will make, if only to satisfy their need to be sure of themselves.

It is what we lack in ourselves that agitates us. What we do not have in our own hearts, we will always look for someplace else. What we do not cultivate within ourselves, we will always demand from others. If we have not learned how to live a rich inner life, we will want the tinsel and glitter of the world around us and someone else's money to get it. If we have not set ourselves to the task of self-development, we will want without end someone else's skills, someone else's gifts, someone else's advantages. If we are insecure, we will demand the control of others. If we have not come to peace with our own life, we will make combat with the people around us. If we have not learned to listen to our own struggles, we will never have compassion on the struggles of others.

Peace comes when we know that there is something that the Spirit has to teach us in everything we do, in everything we experience. When we are rejected, we learn that there is a love above all loves in life. When we are afraid, we come to know that there are those who will take care of us whatever the cost to themselves. When we are lonely, we learn that there is a rich and vibrant world inside of us waiting to be explored if we will only make the effort. When we are threatened by differences, we come to realize that the gift of the other is grace in disguise meant to broaden the narrowness that constricts our souls. Then peace comes, then quiet sets in; then there is nothing that anyone can do to us that can destroy our equilibrium, upset our inner balance. What is, is, that's true. But what is, we come to see, is that God's world is good in all its dimensions. When I finally plumb my own depths, take the measure of myself, find the world within me that is spirit and light and truth, what is outside of me can never destroy my centered self.

The desire for conquest comes, then, when we believe that we already know everything there is to know about the world around us and set out to shape it to those limited assessments. Then it is my will against the world. My wants rage against the needs of the universe. Then the differences I see in others begin to be a threat to my own well-being rather than a promise of inspiring new possibilities and daring new experiences in life. To make ourselves feel a security we do not have, we set out to shape the world to our own small selves.

We rape the planet and make war against peoples and build our private walls higher and higher. We pout and stamp our feet and fly in fear from the very things that stand to draw us out of ourselves and into God. Then we begin to traffic in force rather than in strength. With no center from which to respond we begin to flail madly in the wind, agitated, distracted, unnerved. We become the war makers of our private little worlds. To satisfy our need to feel good about ourselves, we lump people into castes and nations into categories, pitting races and sexes, religions and cultures against one another for our own ends. We entomb ourselves in ourselves. Serbs remain the enemy, Jews stay a mystery to us, strong women disturb our world view, the children of this generation become the enemies of the next. We make war everywhere, both inside of us and out. The question is, then, what is the way to the beginning of peace?

The philosopher Blaise Pascal wrote, "The unhappiness of a person resides in one thing, to be unable to remain peacefully in a room." It is silence and solitude that bring us face to face with ourselves and the inner wars we must win if we are ever to become truly whole, truly at peace. Silence gives us the opportunity we need to raise our hearts and minds to something above ourselves, to be aware of a spiritual life in us that is being starved out by noise pollution, to still the raging of our limitless desires. It is a call to the Cave of the Heart where the vision is clear and the heart is centered on something worthy of it.

There are some things in life that deserve to be nourished simply for their own sake. Art is one, music is another, good reading is a third, but the power of the contemplative vision is the greatest of them all. Only those who come to see the world as God sees the world, only those who see through the eyes of God, ever really see the glory of the world, ever really approach the peaceable kingdom, ever find peace in themselves.

Silence is the beginning of peace. It is in silence that we learn that there is more to life than life seems to offer. There is beauty and truth and vision wider than the present and deeper than the past that only silence can discover. Going into ourselves we see the whole world at war within us and begin to end the conflict. To understand ourselves, then, is to understand everyone else as well.

There are two major obstacles, however, to a development of a spirituality of peace. The fear of silence and solitude loom like cliffs in the human psyche. Noise protects us from confronting ourselves, but silence speaks the language of the heart. Silence and solitude are what really bring us into contact both with ourselves and with others. Deep down inside of us reside, in microcosm, all the human hopes and fears, the struggles to control them, the hope to set them free, the peace that comes when we have confronted both the best and the worst in ourselves and found them acceptable.

Silence requires a respect for solitude, however, and solitude is even more frightening than quiet. One of life's greatest lessons is that solitude and loneliness are not the same thing. Loneliness is the sign that something is lacking. The purpose of solitude, on the other hand, is to bring us home to the center of ourselves with such serenity that we could lose everything and, in the end, lose nothing of the fullness of life at all.

Quiet has become a phantom memory in this culture. Some

generations among us have had no experience of it at all. It has been driven out by noise pollution that is endemic, invasive, clamorous. Everywhere. Everyplace. Not simply in New York City. In Small Town, USA, it is blaring every hour of the day. There is Muzak in the elevators and public address systems in the halls and people standing next to you in the hardware store talking loudly on cellular phones and everywhere, everywhere—in offices and restaurants and kitchens and bedrooms—the ubiquitous television spewing talk devoid of thought while people pay no attention at all and shout above it about other things. There are loudspeakers in boats now so the lake is not safe. There are rock concerts in the countryside now so the mountains are not safe. There are telephones in bathrooms now so the shower is not safe. Corporate offices are now beehives of cubicles, cheek by jowl. We don't think anymore; we simply listen. The problem is that we are so deluged with sound that we are accustomed to listening only to things outside of ourselves, however vacuous the message, however pointless the talk.

Silence is the lost art of this society. Clamor and struggle have replaced it. Silence, of course, was once a thing to be dealt with in the human condition. Silence was a given. Men went with the flocks up a lonely mountain for weeks and had to learn to be at peace with themselves. Women worked in the kitchens of the world grinding corn and plucking chickens, deep in thought, attuned to the things around them. Children picked in the fields in long, separated rows, learning young to hear birds and wind and water, weaving their fancies from the materials of the earth. Silence was a friendly part of life, not a deprivation, not a fearsome place to be. People knew that the silence in which they lived as a matter of course was anything but empty. On the contrary. It was full of the self and all its clamor. Silence had things to teach, and silence was a stern taskmaster, full of angels to be wrestled with and demons to be mollified.

Silence stood demanding and somber waiting for attention. The substance of silence, you see, is the awakening soul and that, all the great spiritual writers knew, is something that shallow hearts assiduously avoid. It is one thing to arm wrestle the demons outside of us. It is entirely another to brave the adversaries within. But dare them we must or die only half finished, only partially human, only somewhat grown.

The desert monastics of the third century were very clear about the role of silence in the development of a mature spirituality.

"Elder, give me a word," the seeker begged for direction.

And the holy one said, "My word to you is to go into your cell and your cell will teach you everything."

The answers are within you, in other words. And so are the questions. Your questions. The questions no one can ask of you but you. Everything else in the spiritual life is mere formula, mere exercise. It is the questions and answers that rant within each of us that, in the end, are all that matter. Then we get to know ourselves as no one else knows us. Then we blush at what we see. And lose our righteousness. And come to peace.

For those who cringe from silence like the plague, fearful of its weight, cautious of its emptiness, the shock that comes with the revelations of silence goes deep. The heaviness and emptiness we feared give way very quickly to turmoil and internal pressure. Silence enables us to hear the cacophony inside ourselves. Being alone with ourselves is a demanding presence. We find very quickly that either we must change or we shall surely crumble under the weight of our own dissatisfaction with ourselves, under the awareness of what we could be but are not, under the impulse of what we want to be but have failed to become. Under the din is the raw material of the soul. Under the din is self-knowledge, is self-acceptance, is peace.

Silence does more than confront us with ourselves, however. Silence makes us wise. Face to face with ourselves we come very quickly, if we listen to the undercurrents that are in contention within us, to respect the struggles of others. Silence teaches us how much we have yet to learn. Or, as we get older, silence perhaps reminds us too that there are qualities that we may never with confidence attain and that will war for our souls till the day we die. Then face to face with our struggles and our inadequacies, there is no room in us for mean judgments and narrow evaluations of others. Suddenly, out of silence, comes the honesty that tempers arrogance and makes us kind.

Because we have come to know ourselves better, we can only deal more gently with others. Knowing our own struggles, we reverence theirs. Knowing our own failures, we are in awe of their successes, less quick to condemn, less likely to boast, less intent on punishing, less certain of our certainties, less committed to our heady, vacuous, and untried convictions. Then silence becomes a social virtue.

Make no doubt about it, the ability to listen to another, to sit silently in the presence of God, to give sober heed and to ponder is the nucleus of the spirituality of peace. It may, in fact, be what is most missing in a century saturated with information, sated with noise, smothered in struggle, but short on reflection. The Word we seek is speaking in the silence within us. Blocking it out with the static of nonsense day in and day out, relinquishing the spirit of silence, anesthetizes the heart in a noise-numbed world and destroys our peace.

An ancient wrote: "Once upon a time a disciple asked the elder, 'How shall I experience my oneness with creation?'"

And the elder answered, "By listening."

The disciple pressed the point: "But how am I to listen?"

And the elder taught, "Become an ear that pays attention to every single thing the universe is saying. The moment you hear something you yourself are saying, stop."

Peace will come when we stretch our minds to listen to the noise within us that needs quieting and the wisdom from outside ourselves that needs to be learned. Then we will have something of value to leave the children besides hate, besides war, besides turmoil. Then peace will come. Then we will be able to say with Kazantzakis, "I fear nothing. I hope for nothing. I am free."

A Time for
Every Purpose under
Heaven

Time, the wag wrote on the wall, is nature's way of preventing everything from happening at once. Maybe all the philosophy in the world was graffiti once upon a time. If not, this piece of graffiti qualifies as high philosophy nevertheless. The truth of it stills the soul for a moment, gives us pause, awakens us to the truth of the temporal in the spiritual development of a person. Time carries us from situation to situation in life, one by one, until eventually we have lived them all. The measure of a life, however, is not whether we have spent our particular number of allotted days but whether in the spending of them we have lived life to the fullest as we went along. But what, precisely, does that mean?

Living life well is akin to paddling a rowboat in an ocean. We have a choice. We can go into the water and fight each passing wave, resist each undertow, confront each swell, fight each current until we break apart, or we can give ourselves to the water to be tossed by it and swept along by it and massaged by it and pummeled by it until, exhausted, we find ourselves beached at that place we had hoped to arrive.

Life is a wild and mesmerizing melody. To live life well, we can join the dance of life, move to its magical music, be moved by its rhythm for us, sing its plaintive songs, or we can sit sullen and watch it all go by, forever a stranger to the cadence it requires of us and the multiple keys it challenges us to reach. In either case we can go with the flow or we can resist it all the way to the bitter end. We can learn from it or reject it completely. There is only one thing we cannot do in life; we cannot ignore its lessons.

Life is a relentless teacher. And life teaches relentlessly.

The lesson we like least to deal with, however, the message we most reject, the concept we will not accept looms large in Ecclesiastes. If there is no other meaning at all to the book, it is surely this: life is not even, life is not smooth. All of these things— birth and death, loving and laughing, gaining and losing— will happen in every life. They are life. We will not be able to avoid them. We will not be so clever as to evade and elude each or any element of them. No, the purpose of life does not rest in dwarfing life to the size of our dwarfed selves. The purpose of life lies in learning to enjoy each giddy part, to endure each costly effort, to cope with every exhausting hurdle, to learn from every colorless segment, to stretch and groan and grow, to milk it dry.

All our efforts to control life, to nail it down to our specifications, to stop its progress toward death and dying cry "Nonsense" to the really wise. When we live out of time—when we insist on being forty in our sixties, and a teenager in our middle years, half-dead as a young wife and mother, an adolescent as a middle-aged man—we mock the now. We miss the moment.

We can't cage life. We cannot freeze the present happy day

under glass. We can't impale it like a butterfly in a frame. No, life moves inexorably on, whether we go with it or not. It rocks and lurches and limps along. It reels from high to low at a pace often too wild to follow, sometimes slow to bear. Whatever it is, life is not an exercise in mental cryonics. We were not born to collect "peak experiences." We were born to remember the few great moments we will have so that dull days, when they come as come they must, do not damp our spirits to the point of living death.

The myth of life lived on an even keel persists in the minds of many, but seduces only the weak of heart. The stalwart know that real life demands a better stamina. Young widows know life's sting. Old inventors know its zest. Middle-aged women know its allure. Young couples know its excitement. Middle-aged men know its false promise. Children know its partiality, that many thrive some of the time and that some struggle ceaselessly.

Through it all, whatever its twists and turns along the way, life leaves us an image burned in our hearts of the serene elderly, the sage and the mature, the ones who fought the fight and found it energizing, the wise whose wisdom engraved itself in gentleness, the strong who learned how to lose. Clearly, at the end of the day, life stands out exceedingly kind. If we do not resist it, if we dance the dance whole and entire, we too may come to the end of it weathered and strong, winsome and laughing, stomping and reeling in holy hysteria for what we have learned, for what we have become that we could not have been without our own particular recipe of cleansing pain and perfect joy in proper proportions.

In the centrifuge of life, forces operate around us and on us over which we have no control. Like pottery, the only one of the arts in which the artist surrenders the final step of the creative process over to the force beyond control, the fire of the kiln, the heat of life that we ourselves withstand will account for our final shape and gleam. Our life not only happens to us, it happens in us, it happens on us, it happens despite us, and it happens because of us. The dynamics of life depend both on what we bring to them and what we take from them. There is no such thing as a meaningless moment.

Life is a growing thing going from seed to sapling, from pillar to post, hither and yon, forwards and backwards but always, always toward its purpose, the shaping of the self into a person of quality, compassion, and joy. For that to happen, every smallest segment must be faced and cannot be fled. Life is not controllable; it is only doable.

Therefore, the keeping of the beat of life, the getting to the marrow of each of its measures, all of its elements is what the dance of life is really all about. Who has lived well? Those who have sucked the juice of life from every period of its growing. Who is the happy person? Those who have survived each of these elements and found themselves to be more human, more wise, more kindly, more just, more flexible, more integrated because of having lived through that period of time, that moment of definition, that phase of survival, that streak of chastening awareness.

No doubt about it, the cycle of time shapes and reshapes our misshapen selves until we have the opportunity to become what we can.

There is a time to kill whatever it is within us that fetters our souls from flying free. It will take patience and terrible doses of truth but, for those who persist, the picture is a pretty one whose promises know no ends.

There is a time to refrain from embracing the patterns of thought, the conventions of life that smother the soul. Living in the Eye of God demands a clearer vision and a truer course.

There is a time to sow the seeds that will be reaped only by the next generation, perhaps, but that are called for now. Sowers face a wary welcome from the satisfied of the world, but sow we must if the new world is ever to come to fruit.

There is a time to weep tears of pain and tears of loss to dignify the going of those things and people in life who have brought us to where we are. There are even times to lament the present, not to wallow in it surely but to muster the energy it takes to change it.

There is a time to embrace the goods of our life with great, thumping hugs that burst our bodies and fill our hearts with light. These are the moments that give fuel for the journey and glimpses of its value.

There is a time to reap, to work without stint and produce without pay, if necessary, so that what must be done can be done in life. Only those who do the arduous work of developing the hard things of the present give us any hope for garnering the future at all. "It is not your obligation to complete your work," the Talmud teaches, "but you are not at liberty to quit it."

There is a time to glory in the gains of life, to run through life head up and lusty, gathering as we go, piling up its goods and laughing all the way. Then, and only then, do all the other moments make sense. Then life shows its gold side, and any amount of exertion is possible after that.

There is a time of love, a time to find ourselves in someone else so that we can find ourselves at all. Love connects us to the rest of the world. Once we have loved anyone at all, it is more difficult to hate. Love mellows us and sets us free of ourselves.

There is a time to lose, a time to let go of whatever has become our captor in life. Losing sucks the center out of the soul and gives us the chance to start again. It is raw time and true time. It tells us a great deal about ourselves and even more about the essentials of life.

There is a time to be born fresh and full, out of the old ideas, the old forms, the old shapes. There is a time to begin again, to look more to where we're going than to where we've been.

There is a time to laugh, to let go of the propriety and old pomposities and join the bungling, lunging, silly human race. We put ourselves at risk when we laugh but come out saner than we were before the burst of insight that humor brings.

There is a time to die, to put an end to things, to stop the carrousel, to surrender to the forces of time and trust. Only when we are willing to let things die in life can things really begin for us. To die a little every day to the old, the useless, the long loved but long gone, is one of life's major achievements. "I have died so little today, friend," Thomas Lux wrote. "Forgive me."

There is a time of war, of struggling against the forces that make for destruction and grind people into estimates of "collateral damage" and forget the commandments of life in their pursuit of the technology of death. "What the world expects of Christians is that they should speak out, loud and clear. . . . They should get away from abstraction and confront the bloodstained face history has taken on today," Camus warns. That is our war. This is our time to wage it.

There is a time to heal ourselves from the hurts that weigh us down and keep us from taking charge of our own lives. To give ourselves over to the reactions of others, to make our own good feeling depend on theirs leaves us at the mercy of misery. Life is for the living, and until we can heal ourselves, we can never really be healthy.

There is a time to build up, to construct the new world, to co-create the globe so that what we leave behind is better than what we have received. In a world of misery and poverty, starvation and oppression, patriarchy and militarism, builders are in short supply, rare finds and precious to the ultimate.

There is a time for peace, for coming to grips with the demons within us, for staring them down and smoothing them out, so that we can spread peace like velvet and live peace like feathers and become peace like a fragrance that knows no bounds.

And who shall do all these things? Ecclesiastes is very clear on the point: you and I have no choice; the task is ours. By its very definition life demands it of us. And are the likes of us up to such valor when the great ones who have gone before us did not, it seems, accomplish all the work themselves? The rabbis leave no doubt about the answer:

"How can someone as lowly as I possibly live like Moses?" the disciple Zyusha asked.

"When you die," the rabbi answered, "you will not be asked, 'Why were you not Moses?' You will be asked, 'Why were you not Zyusha?'"

The season is now. The time is ours.